IF GOD WILLS

BRINGING THE CRESCENT TO THE CROSS

Kent Philpott

EVP

Earthen Vessel Publishing

If God Wills

ISBN: 978-0-9968590-4-2
Also published under the title,
    If Allah Wills, ISBN: 978-0-9907277-5-0

Cover and interior design by KLC Philpott

All Biblical Scripture quotations, unless otherwise indicated, are
taken from the Holy Bible, English Standard Version® (ESV®),
copyright © 2001 by Crossway Bibles, a publishing ministry of
Good News Publishers. All rights reserved.

All Qur'an quotations are taken from
The Holy Qur'an. 10th ed. Translated by Abdullah Yusuf Ali.
New Delhi: Kitab Bhavan, 2015.

DEDICATION

If God Wills is dedicated to my Muslim friends, neighbors, and all seekers after the Creator who has made us all in His image and loves us with an everlasting love.

CONTENTS

PREFACE

For many years I was on my guard against Muslim people, due to the constant stream of news stories about bombings, beheadings, and other terrible things happening in Muslim countries and perpetrated by Muslims. I could not feel good about what was going on.

Beginning in 2001, I began to study Islam. The essays I wrote at that time took on the character of warnings of what Islam was all about and what its global intentions were.

However, things changed for me a little over a year ago. It might sound odd, but to put it simply, God gave me a love for Muslim people. No, I did not get warm and fuzzy about the extremist violence I read of in the newspapers, nor did I change my politics, which have always tended toward moderation and toleration. But something fundamental took place within my heart, all while I was teaching a course on Islam at the church where I am a Christian pastor. For the first time I found myself motivated by a love for Muslims and a desire to cross the divide between our two faiths.

Muslims, like people the world over, want to live and let live. Yet something awful is happening. I believe that an internal mechanism in the religion itself is flawed. What it is precisely I am not sure, but something hideous has taken over the religion, just as has occurred at various points in history in other religions of the world, including Christianity. No human or human institution is pure and perfect. This must be admitted, or we become trapped in a dangerous mindset that can only be labeled cultic.

Now I have something in my heart and mind toward Muslim people that will not let me go. I call it love. It certainly was never present in me before, and I can only think that God put it there. This book is the result of that love.

My hope is that Christians who also have a heart for Muslim people are reading this book, and perhaps more Christians than Muslims will read this book. But I suspect that some Muslims will want to read and examine what I have to say, as we can all agree that truth is paramount. We do not want to be duped, especially when heaven or hell is at stake. "Is what I believe true?" is a question that mature and secure people will ask. After all, the Day of Judgment is coming.

My hope is that I will not offend, but rather challenge my readers to think and reflect on matters of extreme importance. Indeed, I honestly and openly invite Muslims to examine their core beliefs.

WHY I AM WRITING THIS BOOK

My intention is to present something other than what is contained in the steady flow of materials on Islam, some of it downright fear-mongering, so that dialogue with Muslims can be carried on in an atmosphere of mutual respect. I wish to challenge Muslims who are willing to engage, to learn from them, and to share my faith in Jesus with them. I hope this book will increase opportunities for myself and for other Christians and non-affiliated persons to do just that.

My credentials are simply that I have read what I could, talked with whom I could, thought through what I learned, and struggled to write this piece. I have my college and seminary degrees, I have been a pastor for over forty-five years, and I have written prolifically on a wide variety of subjects.

I am not writing from a political point of view. I am pro-Israel and pro-Palestinian, both at once. I try hard not to be an extremist, left or right, up or down. My world view is taken from John 3:16: "For God so loved the world that he gave his only son, that whoever believes in him should not perish but have eternal life." Muslims are part of that "world" that God loves so much.

Most Muslims know a lot about Islam, but not much about Jesus Christ, except what is found in the Qur'an itself. The Jesus of the Qur'an is portrayed in a positive manner, mostly. My sense of it is that some Muslims will be willing to consider learning more.

Lastly, I invite communication from Muslims. Let us debate and converse about the really large issues in life, considering that eternal realities are at issue. My email address is:
philpott.kent@yahoo.com

To my Christian audience: Throughout this book, the word "Allah" is used to denote the concept of the Creator God in the world of Islam. This is only proper, considering that many comparisons will be presented in which "God" and "Allah" will be discussed both separately, together, and in an overlapping manner. Consider that you are learning how to speak to your Muslim friend in terms understandable to Muslims rather than compromising your own understanding.

INTRODUCTION

IF ALLAH WILLS

If Allah Wills, or *insha'allah*, is a phrase common to Islam. It comes from Sura Al Kahf (18): 23–24, which says, "And never say of anything 'I shall do such and such thing tomorrow.' Except (with the saying): 'If God wills!'"

IF

The "if" is an intriguing idea, as it suggests various possibilities. One might, or might not "will." One might "will" at one moment and not at another. "If" has both a past and future component. "If" carries the possibility that there may be new information just around the corner.

ALLAH

"Allah" is a name used for the Creator of the entire universe and was used by Christians and Jews in the Middle East for centuries before the birth of Muhammad. That Muhammad used it is only natural. The name is one thing; the nature and character of Allah is another, of course. For Muslims Allah is mono, singular, and only one. He is the one who has created all things, given the world the Qur'an, and sent Muhammad as his final prophet. He needs no partner and has no son.

For many Christians "Allah" is the word used to describe the Creator God as revealed in the Bible as Father, Son, and Holy Spirit, a three-in-one called "Trinity," each member having the exact same will, being, and nature—thus a unified One.

There are some Christians who think it is not proper to use Allah as the name for God, and on this point we must agree to disagree. I will be using the names Allah and God both interchangeably as well as separately. I recognize our commonality of reverence for the Creator and Supreme Being, whichever name we use for him.

WILLS

"Wills" means for most Muslims that whatever comes to pass is the will of Allah. This notion may lack an actual ethic, although the Qur'an and the Hadith are full of **pro**scriptions, meaning that which is forbidden, and **pre**scriptions, meaning that which is permitted, even commanded. The will of Allah is the trump card—the overarching determiner—and all things that actually happen therefore must be or have been the will of Allah.

A CALL TO HUMILITY

Taken together, the phrase *If Allah Wills* suggests a humble approach to the things of God. It must be admitted that we are not aware of all that Allah wills, nor is it always easy to discern what his will is. What we do understand is that seeking the will of God and submitting to it is the chief concern for all human beings.

AN APPEAL TO QUR'AN 29:46

I am writing as a Christian, a follower of Jesus Christ. For me, Surah 29 and verse 46 of the Qur'an is incredibly important:

And dispute ye not
With the People of the Book,
Except with means better
(Than mere disputation), unless
It be with those of them
Who inflict wrong (and injury);
But say, "We believe
In the Revelation which has
Come down to us and in that
Which came down to you;
Our God and your God
Is One; and it is to Him
We bow (in Islam)."

Qur'an 3:84 corroborates the message of Surah 29:46:

Say: "We believe
In God, and in what
Has been revealed to us
And what was revealed
To Abraham, Isma'il,
Isaac, Jacob, and The Tribes,
And in (the Books)
Given to Moses, Jesus,
And the Prophets,
From their Lord:
We make no distinction
Between one and another
Among them, and to God do we
Bow our will (in Islam)."

Based on these two verses from the Qur'an, what Jesus and the Christians teach was accepted by Muhammad. However, this does not prove to be the case for Islam today, since the core of what Christians call the Gospel has been denied by

Islam. Christians may rightfully respond by thinking, "What are we to do with this contradiction?"

REPLACEMENT?

"Abrogation" is a concept integral to Islam. It means that earlier revelations given to Muhammad and recorded in the Qur'an are repealed or replaced by later revelations and verses. In regard to the verses in the Qur'an that commend the People of the Book and recommend that their Books be accepted, as we read above, these are replaced, or abrogated, by later revelations by Allah given to Muhammad. This means that Allah's will can change, and suggests it may change again. With this in mind, perhaps it is not farfetched to suppose that Allah may once again will for Muslims to consider the message of Jesus, as Muhammad once did.

Here is what Jesus said about the will of Allah, as reported in John 6:38–40:

> *"For I have come down from heaven, not to do my own will but the will of him who sent me."*
>
> *"And this is the will of him who sent me, that I should lose nothing of all that he has given me, but raise it up on the last day."*
>
> *"For this is the will of my Father, that everyone who looks on the son and believes in him should have eternal life, and I will raise him up on the last day."*

THREE FORMS THAT MAKE UP THIS BOOK

There are fifteen chapters in this book, interspersed with either an "Appeal" or a "Contrast."

In the **Appeals**, I am asking Muslim readers to help clarify some point of interest.

The **Contrasts** are invitations to Muslim readers to consider Christian concepts, ideas, or doctrines as they compare to Muslim ideas.

The whole point is to be interactive with the reader, to engage through questions, challenges, and juxtapositions.

My central appeal is that those who read this book will keep an open mind and that together we might seek God in prayer, asking him to reveal his will to us, even if it means a complete revolution in our hearts and minds.

If Allah wills, we will find a meaningful meeting place based on mutual respect, curiosity, honesty, and shared love of God.

ONE

TAWHID

If **Allah wills**, we may join hearts and minds on this major topic and in the process make discoveries that will be of great importance. Christians and Muslims both want the same thing, which is to know the truth and be in heaven with God forever.

Tawhid sits at the heart of the matter. To my Muslim readers I ask: Could *Tawhid* and Trinity mean the same thing?

TAWHID

Tawhid is the central affirmation of Islamic theology. Muhammad preached against polytheism at the very outset of his work. At the *Kaaba* he denounced the worship of many gods and proclaimed that Allah was the one and only God.

Tawhid is the oneness of God. *Tawhid* means there is no God apart from Allah and Allah has no partner and no son.

The God of the Christian Bible is also One.

Let us look at a prophecy from ca. 750 BCE in Isaiah 45:21:

Declare and present your case; let them take counsel together! Who told this long ago? Who declared it of old? Was it not I, the LORD? And there is no other god besides me, a righteous God and a Savior; there is none besides me.

Another declaration of *Tawhid* almost twice as ancient is found in Deuteronomy 6:4: "Hear, O Israel: The LORD our God, the LORD is one." Moses rejected the polytheism he found in Egypt, and Isaiah likewise denounced it in the land of Canaan where the Jews later lived, that place called The Promised Land.

Muhammad made the same judgment. Found in the first words of the *Shahada* is, "There is only God worthy of worship." This is what *Tawhid* is all about: the oneness of Allah.

Different forms of *Tawhid* can be identified in Islamic thought, such as *Tawhid ar-rububiya*, or the *Tawhid* of lordship; *Tawhid al-uluhiya*, or the *Tawhid* of worship; and *Tawhid al-Asma was-Sifaat*, or the *Tawhid* of Allah's names and attributes.

The negation of *Tawhid* is the unforgivable sin known as shirk.

TRINITY

Christians believe in the declarations of Isaiah 45:21 and Deuteronomy 6:4 about the oneness of God. We worship only one God.

However, Muslims consider the Christian Trinity to be polytheistic—the worship of more than one God.

Muhammad stated that Christians worship the Father, a son, and Mary, the mother of the son, Jesus. This is a misunderstanding of the Trinity.

THE TRIUNE GOD

Qur'an Al'Imran 3:84 reads:

> *Say: "We believe*
> *In God, and in what*

Has been revealed to us
And what was revealed
To Abraham, Isma'il;
Isaac, Jacob, and the Tribes
And in (the Books)
Given to Moses, Jesus,
And the Prophets,
From their Lord:
We make no distinction
Between one and another
Among them, and to God do we
Bow our will (in Islam)."

The prophets of Israel reveal that the longed-for Messiah is God himself. Let's take this opportunity to look more closely at one of those prophets and what he said about the Messiah.

Isaiah 7:14 states, "Therefore the Lord himself will give you a sign. Behold, the virgin shall conceive and bear a son, and shall call his name Immanuel." Immanuel is a Hebrew word that means, "God with us." It indicates that the child born to the virgin is literally God born in the flesh.

Isaiah 9:6–7 continues the account of the son of the virgin:

For to us a child is born, to us a son is given; and the government shall be upon his shoulder, and his name shall be called Wonderful Counselor, Mighty God, Everlasting Father, Prince of Peace. Of the increase of his government and of peace there will be no end, on the throne of David and over his kingdom, to establish it and to uphold it with justice and with righteousness from this time forth and forevermore. The zeal of the LORD of hosts will do this.

Consider the "virgin"—a woman who had never had sexual relations with a man. The "zeal" of the LORD would be the supernatural means of the conception, and not a sexual relationship. The idea that God would have sexual relations with a human being is abhorrent to Christians, as it was to the ancient Hebrews. Muhammad was right to declare that this was blasphemous.

Jesus was the one born of a virgin. When the angel Gabriel appeared to Mary and told her she would have a child, Mary could not believe it, because she had never been with a man.

Here is the condensed story from Luke 1:28–33:

> *And he* [the angel Gabriel] *came to her and said, "Greetings, O favored one, the Lord is with you!"* ... [Mary was troubled, so Gabriel said,] *"Do not be afraid, Mary. ... And behold, you will conceive in your womb and bear a son, and you shall call his name Jesus. He will be great and will be called the Son of the Most High. And the Lord God will give to him the throne of his father David, and he will reign over the house of Jacob forever, and of his kingdom there will be no end."*

(Note that this is Gabriel speaking, the same angel through whom Islam says Allah spoke to Muhammad.)

Gabriel said the Son to be born was descended from "his father David," who was the king of Israel 1,000 years earlier. Therefore, we see that the words were not to be taken literally, but had symbolic meaning for the Jewish people and later for Christians as well. Jesus was not literally born from David. Instead, Jesus would be born in the **lineage** of David, and the genealogies found in the Gospel accounts from both Matthew and Luke corroborate this.

Mary's son was God—God in the flesh—in fulfillment of Isaiah's prophecy some 750 years earlier. Jesus is God the Son.

The Holy Spirit is God as well. We see this in many places in the Bible, even as early as the second verse of Genesis, where we read, "The earth was without form and void, and darkness was over the face of the deep. And the Spirit of God was hovering over the face of the waters."

Christians do not view God as Father only, but also as Son and Holy Spirit, each with the exact same nature, mind, heart, and will. They are what the Hebrew Bible describes as an *echad*, a plurality in unity.

To understand *echad* more fully, let's look at Genesis 2:24. God created a man and a woman, Adam and Eve, and described the process by which they become an *echad*: "Therefore a man shall leave his father and his mother and hold fast to his wife, and they shall become one flesh." In this verse, the word "one" in Hebrew is *echad*. The man and woman become one as a married couple—an *echad*. There are other Hebrew words that could have been used that mean a singular entity. Instead the plurality in unity, *echad*, is used.

Perhaps the analogy of a "team" could be used to illustrate *echad*. A baseball team has nine players, but it is a single team. In the same way, the Trinity is one yet three. This analogy has its limits, as a baseball team is made of nine persons. "Person" is a word that is not used in the Bible to describe the Trinity. If the Bible did use the word "person," that would lend support to the Trinity being three separate persons. Councils of the Church convened centuries after the Bible was written and settled on the word "person" in their definitions of the Trinity. This may have been a confusing choice of words, and it is not Biblically accurate.

John the Apostle said of Jesus, "In the beginning was the Word, and the Word was with God, and the Word was God" (John 1:1). Jesus is understood as being the Word of God. Another way of understanding the meaning of the ancient Greek text is to say, "The Word was and is in the beginning, and God was and is with the Word, and God was and is the Word." We want to also note that the word "with" means exact sameness.

John continues in verse 14 of the same chapter: "And the Word became flesh and dwelt among us, and we have seen his glory, glory as of the only Son from the Father, full of grace and truth." Notice the phrase, "only Son." The Greek word means "the one unique one." No one else ever was or ever will be like this Son.

Some say Jesus never claimed to be God, but in John 10:30 Jesus said, "I and the Father are one." Here we see something of the mystery of the Trinity. Jesus is fully God and also fully man, which is the ultimate paradox from a human point of view. But nothing is impossible for God.

The Trinity is Father, Son, and Holy Spirit: One God. Thus I propose that the Christian view of God meets the definition of *Tawhid*.

"SON OF MAN" AND "SON OF GOD"

The above terms that are used of Jesus, and by Jesus himself to refer to his own person, cause problems for Muslims and understandably so.

The words, as understood by most people, if taken literally, would imply that God had sex with a human woman and produced a child. Such would be truly problematic and would be considered blasphemous for not only Muslims but for Christians and Jews as well.

However, the terms "Son of God" and "Son of Man" are not to be taken literally but are code words or symbols for Messiah or Christ. Messiah from the Hebrew or Aramaic and Christ from the Greek mean the "**Anointed One**," that One sent forth by God the Creator as his single and authoritative representative. The term comes close to meaning "exalted and only King." Kings and priests were anointed by prophets, as we see in the books of Leviticus and 1 Samuel.

The first sermon or teaching Jesus ever delivered came in the synagogue at Nazareth. There Jesus was handed the scroll containing the prophecy of Isaiah from which he read Isaiah 61:1–2:

> *The Spirit of the Lord is upon me, because he has anointed me to proclaim good news to the poor. He has sent me to*

proclaim liberty to the captives and recovering of sight to the blind, to set at liberty those who are oppressed, to proclaim the year of the Lord's favor. (Luke 4:18–19)

We must be clear; when Christians use the term "Son of Man" or "Son of God" we mean that Jesus Christ is the Anointed One or Messiah. In no way whatsoever is it meant that God had sex with a woman and produced a son. That Muhammad said the opposite does not negate the actual meaning of the historical terms.

EVEN DEMONS BELIEVE

Demons know all about *Tawhid*. They believe it, as they should, since it is the truth. James, the half-brother of Jesus, put it this way: "You believe that God is one; you do well. Even the demons believe—and shudder!" (James 2:19).

Satan and his demons do not know all things, but they know basic facts, such as who Jesus is. When Jesus confronted a demon-possessed man in a synagogue in Capernaum, here is what the demon said: "What have you to do with us, Jesus of Nazareth? Have you come to destroy us? I know who you are—the Holy One of God" (Mark 1:24).

Polytheism is a corruption of the true knowledge of God. The demons know this, and so do Christians.

Dear Muslim friends, please know that Christians believe in one God and thus do not violate the principle of Tawhid. We are not polytheists.

If Allah wills, may he reveal the truth to those who seek after him and call upon his name.

MUHAMMAD AND JESUS

Muhammad must not be worshipped alongside Allah; to do so would be idolatry, since Muhammad is but a man: he is a guide, a warner, and a messenger, but not an angel or deity of any kind.

How does this compare with the way Jesus is regarded in the *Injil* (the New Testament, including the four Gospels)? Jesus is worshiped based on who he is; he is considered to be God in the flesh.

IS MUHAMMAD WORSHIPED?

Muslims emulate the behavior and life of Muhammad. They revere Muhammad's life and use it as an example of how they should live. Is it not the desire of all Muslims to eat like he did, for the men to grow a beard like his, to have many wives as he did, to dress like him, and to advance Islam just as Muhammad did?

Is Muhammad worshiped? As I read the *hadith* and the *sira* (the biography of Muhammad), it seems so. Yet only God can be worshiped—otherwise we are committing blasphemy and are polytheists.

IS JESUS WORSHIPED?

Among Christians Jesus is worshiped, followed, and loved, without fear of blasphemy, since Jesus is considered God, sent to be with us in human form.

Most Christians do not attempt to eat like, look like, or dress like Jesus. But we do follow him and aspire to be like him. He is meek and lowly in heart, loving the sinner, and full of compassion and forgiveness. While dying on the cross he even asked the Father in heaven to forgive those who were crucifying him. Here is what Jesus actually said about those responsible for his execution: "Father, forgive them, for they know not what they do" (Luke 23:34).

THE CONTRAST

The contrast between the worship of Jesus and of Muhammad could not be greater. Islam denies Muhammad is God, and yet seems to worship him while denying the deity of Jesus. Christians deny the deity of Muhammad, while affirming the deity of Jesus and worshiping him as the God-man.

Jesus knew who he was and stated plainly "I and the Father are one" (John 10:30). He predicted that he would be crucified, would die, be buried, and that he would be raised from the dead. Then he would be seated at the right hand of the Father in heaven and would come again at the end of the age, the Day of Judgment.

Muhammad, on the other hand, was uncertain about his own destiny to the point he did not know if he would even enter Paradise. Qur'an Al-Ahqaf 46:9 makes this clear:

> *Say; "I am no bringer*
> *Of new-fangled doctrine*
> *Among the apostles, nor*
> *Do I know what will*
> *Be done with me or*
> *With you. I follow*

But that which is revealed
To me by inspiration;
I am but a Warner
Open and clear."

Here is the way Jesus spoke of the end of the age:

Then will appear in heaven the sign of the Son of Man and then all the tribes of the earth will mourn, and they will see the Son of Man coming on the clouds of heaven with power and great glory. And he will send out his angels with a loud trumpet call, and they will gather his elect from the four winds, from one end of heaven to the other. (Matthew 24:30–31)

TWO

GABRIEL

The name "Gabriel" comes to us from the ancient Hebrew language and means, "God is mighty." The word "angel" means messenger, and so we understand the angel Gabriel to be a divine messenger sent from God.

There are four verses in the Bible in which the angel Gabriel is mentioned. In Daniel 8:16 and 9:21, Gabriel reveals events that were to take place in the future; in Luke 1:19-20, Gabriel reveals to the priest Zechariah that he was to be the father of John the Baptist. In Luke 1:26-37, Gabriel reveals to Mary that she would give birth to the Messiah of Israel.

Upon first encountering the angel Gabriel, Daniel, Zechariah, and Mary were each frightened at his appearance, but Gabriel quickly reassured them, and each was then able to communicate with the angel without further fear.

The angel that appeared to Muhammad at a cave on the slopes of Mount Hirah was very different in character from the one who appeared in the Bible. Muhammad's angel "pressed" him so severely that he was left questioning whether what he encountered was from God at all. Muhammad's wife Khadija argued persuasively that the being was in fact from God.

GABRIEL AND DANIEL

Daniel was taken to Babylon as a young man in 605 BCE and served in the court of Nebuchadnezzar. After the Persians overcame Babylon in 539 BCE, Daniel, now an old man, served God and came to the attention of the Persian leaders. Through Daniel God brought visions of what would take place in the future. A simple reading of history shows Daniel's prophecies to be accurate.

The angel Gabriel was the servant of God who brought messages to Daniel.

GABRIEL AND ZECHARIAH

Zechariah was serving the Lord as a Levitical priest in the temple in Jerusalem several months before the birth of Jesus. The angel Gabriel appeared to him to announce that his prayers for his barren wife Elizabeth were heard and that she would soon become pregnant.

Gabriel explained that this son, John the Baptist, would prepare the way for one who would come after him. This long-awaited one was to "turn many of the children of Israel to the Lord their God" (Luke 1:16). This is clearly a reference to Jesus.

GABRIEL AND MARY

Mary, the young virgin, found favor with God. This is the only reason given in Scripture for the high place this insignificant Jewish girl plays in human history. The angel Gabriel told her, "'You will conceive in your womb and bear a son, and you shall call his name Jesus'" (Luke 1:31). The name Jesus means "God saves."

Gabriel went on to describe this son: "'He will be great and will be called the Son of the Most High. And the Lord God will give to him the throne of his father David, and he will reign over the house of Jacob forever, and of his kingdom there will be no end'" (Luke 1:32-33).

Mary's conception was to be miraculous, not the result of sexual union. "Son of the Most High" means that the child Mary would bear would be deity.

Mary's response to Gabriel was, "How will this be, since I am a virgin?" (Luke 1:34). Mary understood that the conception was not to be achieved through usual means. Gabriel's answer to Mary was, "The Holy Spirit will come upon you, and the power of the Most High will overshadow you; therefore the child to be born will be called holy—the Son of God" (Luke 1:35).

This is how the great miracle of God prophesied by Isaiah occurred. Mary conceived yet remained a virgin.

WHICH IS THE REAL GABRIEL?

Which Gabriel is the real "angel of God?" The answer to this question has enormous repercussions. Either the Gabriel of the Bible or the Gabriel of the Qur'an is the real angel of God. Both cannot be him.

The words of the angel Gabriel, as recorded in Luke's gospel, cannot be abrogated by a later communication from Muhammad. As an angel, or messenger, Gabriel speaks for God.

Gabriel's words to Mary are an essential element of the Gospel of Jesus Christ. Is it possible that Gabriel changed his mind between his meeting with Mary announcing the soon arrival of God himself in human form sent to save mankind and his later meeting with Muhammad, with a message demoting Jesus and veering from his plan of salvation? Would God change his mind about things of such momentous significance?

THE COURAGE TO QUESTION

Muslims and Christians alike are left to grapple with this dilemma. It is for us to bravely and honestly examine both sides and come to our conclusions. Again, we can appeal to

God to reveal the answer to the question, "which was the real Gabriel?"

For me, the question of Gabriel's true identity was answered when I was twenty-one years old and became a believer in Jesus, and it has been continuously confirmed in the last fifty-two years as a follower of Jesus. For me, Gabriel was the one who proclaimed these deeply encouraging words to the priest Zechariah about his son John the Baptist:

> *And you, child, will be called the prophet of the Most High; for you will go before the Lord to prepare his ways, to give knowledge of salvation to his people in the forgiveness of their sins, because of the tender mercy of our God, whereby the sunrise shall visit us from on high to give light to those who sit in darkness and in the shadow of death, to guide our feet into the way of peace.* (Luke 1:76–79)

If Allah wills, we will discover the truth about who the angel Gabriel really is and what is his essential message to humanity as a messenger of God.

TAQIYYA

This appeal to Muslim readers for clarification and assistance concerns *taqiyya*, which is Arabic for dissimulation and essentially has to do with not telling the truth.

Shi'a Muslims who were facing persecution first developed *taqiyya*. It gave them permission to disguise the fact that they were Muslims in order to save their lives. What began as a remedy for emergency situations became normalized and broadened in scope, perhaps also due to cultural pressures to "save face" and honor.

The principle derives from two passages in Qur'an Al-Baqara and Qur'an An-Nahl:

> *And spend of your substance*
> *In the cause of God,*
> *And make not your own hands*
> *Contribute to (your) destruction;*
> *But do good;*
> *For God loveth those*
> *Who do good. (Qur'an 2:195)*

Any one who, after accepting
Faith in God, utters Unbelief,
Except under compulsion,
His heart remaining firm;
In Faith—But such as
Open their breast to Unbelief,—
On them is Wrath from God,
And theirs will be
A dreadful Penalty. (Qur'an 16:106)

In addition, a number of *hadith* passages are seen as permitting falsehood in three situations: firstly, a man may lie to his wife to please her; secondly, to bring reconciliation between two parties who have quarreled; thirdly, in war, espionage, and other actions against an enemy. For many Muslims the result has been an acceptance of deception across the board.

Former and present Muslims have led me to understand that, for the purpose of glorifying Islam, their altering of facts about Islam's history, contributions to science, math, architecture, and so on, is acceptable and approved, even to the point that such distortion is instantly forgiven by Allah. My own research has confirmed this.

This is an appeal to my Muslim readers to explain how I can engage in honest and open discussions with your religious experts, if *taqiyya* is in operation.

In the Christian faith, lying is considered a sin. Those who seek to become more like Jesus experience an inner pang of conscience when they lie, because it is displeasing to God for us to lie. Honesty is an expression of love, and we are commanded to love one another just as Jesus loves us.

In Islam, when *taqiyya* is practiced, does the speaker who is acting in deceit experience a pang of conscience? Or is there no need for a pang of conscience when Allah has presumably given license to lie? Are such deceivers really considered to be serving the cause of Islam in so doing?

I have found myself more than once in conversation with those who presume I know nothing about Islam and therefore knowingly seek to mislead me. I am troubled by this impediment to true dialogue, and for that reason I make this appeal.

THREE

PARADISE

How can we be sure we will be in paradise? This is the most significant question anyone can hope to answer. Either we will be in paradise or we will be in hell. It will be one or the other, with no other possibility, and both Muslims and Christians hold to this truth.

THE GREAT SCALE

For Muslims, going to paradise depends on believing and on doing right. We picture in our minds the great scale of Allah. On one side of the scale are all our good deeds, on the other all our bad deeds. The good must outweigh the bad.

Yet there is no way to know for certain whether our good deeds outweigh our bad deeds. Even Muhammad himself did not know whether he would enter paradise. If the founder of Islam did not know for certain, how can any Muslim?

Another requirement for paradise is purity. How do we measure purity? The *Salafis* are followers of the pure forefathers; must one live like a *Salafi*? Might even *Salafis* transgress sometimes, even if only in their thoughts? Does one really have to die in jihad to be assured of an eternal home in paradise? Or maybe if one builds a mosque? These are difficult questions, and there are no real answers in the Qur'an or the *hadith*. Muslim scholars differ on these questions.

THE THIEF ON THE CROSS

In the Bible there is an interesting story about two thieves who were crucified alongside Jesus, one on either side of him. (Although Islam teaches that Jesus was not crucified, I ask you to consider this story.)

"One of the criminals who were hanged railed at him, saying, 'Are you not the Christ? Save yourself and us!' " (Luke 23:39). He mocked Jesus, even on the brink of death.

The other thief rebuked the first thief and said to him, "Do you not fear God, since you are under the same sentence of condemnation? And we indeed justly, for we are receiving the due reward of our deeds; but this man has done nothing wrong."

The second thief then turned to Jesus and said, "Jesus, remember me when you come into your kingdom."

Jesus replied, "Truly, I say to you, today you will be with me in paradise" (Luke 23: 40–43).

Jesus died before the other two men, but all died on the same day. Jesus immediately went to paradise, from which he had come to be born of a virgin. According to Jesus, the second thief, although a sinful man, would be with him in paradise that very same day. The only thing required of him was that he believe in Jesus as his Savior. This demonstrates God's amazing love, mercy, and grace.

PARADISE = HEAVEN

"Paradise," a word used long before the days of Muhammad, is derived from Farsi, the language spoken by the Persians. It pictures a perfect world here on planet earth with plenty of food, water, wine, and every earthly delight enjoyed by man.

In Luke's Gospel we find Jesus using the word "paradise," although the word most often used in the Gospels to refer to the abode of God is "heaven." The universe was created by God and did not always exist, and the Bible teaches that it will one day be dissolved (see 2 Peter 3:8–13). The eternal spiritual dwelling place of God is what is meant in the Bible by the words "paradise" and "heaven."

The closing chapters of the Book of Revelation picture a new heaven and a new earth, also referred to as the new Jerusalem. All of the old has passed away, including the universe. All things are made new.

The following is a description of heaven from the Bible:

Then I saw a new heaven and a new earth, for the first heaven and the first earth had passed away, and the sea was no more. And I saw the holy city, new Jerusalem, coming down out of heaven from God, prepared as a bride adorned for her husband. And I heard a loud voice from the throne saying, "Behold, the dwelling place of God is with man. He will dwell with them and they will be his people, and God himself will be with them as their God. He will wipe away every tear from their eyes, and death shall be no more, neither shall there be mourning, nor crying, nor pain anymore, for the former things have passed away." (Revelation 21:1–4)

What is Paradise Like?

The terms "city," "new Jerusalem," even "new heaven and new earth" are symbolic of something so wonderful, pure, and eternal, that it cannot be fully grasped by the human mind. It is dwelling with God forever and ever. All the burdens of our earthly lives are gone. There is no sin or evil there. In God's presence all our needs and desires are fully satisfied.

Neither will there be marriage in heaven. No marrying, nor virgins with whom to have sexual intercourse—no need for fulfillment of our carnal desires. There is no place in heaven for the indulgence of fleshly cravings.

Some religious people in Jesus' day who denied the resurrection and heaven altogether questioned Jesus. His reply is significant: "For in the resurrection they neither marry nor are given in marriage, but are like angels in heaven" (Matthew 22:30).

HOW CAN WE KNOW WE WILL ENTER PARADISE?

Our deepest longing is to be assured that we are going to live in paradise forever.

Here is the assurance Jesus offers: "'I give them eternal life, and they will never perish, and no one will snatch them out of my hand. My father, who has given them to me, is greater than all, and no one is able to snatch them out of the Father's hand'" (John 10:28–29).

The apostle Paul had a personal encounter with the risen Jesus after the resurrection and was given revelation about the identity, character, and redemption plan of Jesus. Here is an insight from Paul regarding our assurance of salvation through Jesus:

> *What then shall we say to these things? If God is for us, who can be against us? He who did not spare his own Son but gave him up for us all, how will he not also with him graciously give us all things? Who shall bring any charge against God's elect? It is God who justifies. Who is to condemn? Christ Jesus is the one who died—more than that, who was raised—who is at the right hand of God, who indeed is interceding for us. Who shall separate us from the love of Christ? Shall tribulation, or distress, or persecution, or famine, or nakedness, or danger, or sword? As it is written, "For your sake we are being killed all the day long; we are regarded as sheep to be slaughtered." No, in all these things we are more than*

conquerors through him who loved us. For I am sure that neither death nor life, nor angels nor rulers, nor things present nor things to come, nor powers, nor height nor depth, nor anything else in all creation, will be able to separate us from the love of God in Christ Jesus our Lord. (Romans 8:31–39)

BLESSED ASSURANCE

Jesus himself is the certainty of our everlasting life in heaven. He took our sin upon himself on the cross, he died and was buried, and all our sin was buried forever as well. He rose from the dead and ascended back to heaven and will come again to judge the living and the dead. His message points to the simplicity of knowing for certain that we can enter paradise and be with God forever, simply by believing in him, as did the thief on the cross.

If Allah wills, you and I will spend eternity in paradise.

ISLAM AND CHRISTIANITY: THE EARLY YEARS

THE EARLY YEARS OF ISLAM

Though some claim that Islam goes back as far as Adam, and that all those throughout history who believed and lived right were Muslims, the actual history of Islam dates back to the seventh century in what is now Saudi Arabia. A claim back to the far antiquity of creation is not supportable historically; it is myth only.

Early on, while Muhammad lived in Mecca, the polytheists he preached against persecuted him. His own tribe was slow to accept the idea that Allah had chosen Muhammad as his apostle and messenger. But over time this changed, and Islam began to grow. As Muhammad pressed his claims further, he ran into resistance and finally moved to Medina in 622 CE. As Muhammad grew stronger, warfare became a vehicle in the expansion of Islam.

In 632 CE Muhammad died without leaving a clear-cut successor. Abu Bakr (632–634) was declared the first caliph or successor to Muhammad. Then followed Umar (634–644) and Uthman (644–656), who were the first leaders of what would become the Sunni branch of Islam. Some claim that

Islam expanded by virtue of trade or commerce and not by force, but objective history does not back this assertion. All of these leaders expanded Islam primarily by force or by various forms of intimidation. In keeping with the violence of Islam's growth, of the three first caliphs only the first died a natural death—Abu Bakr.

On the Shiite side, Ali became the first Imam (656–661), having rejected the title of fourth caliph. He was also assassinated.

It is impossible to view the seventh and eighth centuries as a time of peaceful growth for Islam. It was a time of jihad and constant warfare. While there were periods when Muslims lived in peace with their neighbors, sooner or later a zealous Muslim would arise seeking to return to the glorious era of Islam by way of both the greater and lesser forms of jihad. The traditionalists—*salafi*, *wahhabi*, and extremists of various sorts—have surfaced throughout Islam's history. We cannot look to Islam's history to validate the attribution of the phrase "The Religion of Peace" to Islam.

THE EARLY YEARS OF CHRISTIANITY

The exact beginning of the Christian Church is debated. Some say it began with Adam; others identify Noah, Abraham, or Moses, among others, as the founders of the religion. Most identify the beginning of the Church as the Day of Pentecost in or about the year 33 CE.

The story of that seminal Pentecost day is found in the first chapters of the Book of Acts in the Bible. Approximately 120 disciples were gathered in Jerusalem to celebrate the Jewish Feast of Pentecost, or Weeks, as commanded by God in Leviticus 23:15–22. Pentecost occurs fifty days after Passover and was mandated by God as a thanksgiving for the wheat harvest. Jewish tradition also says that the Law was given to Moses at Mt. Sinai on Pentecost.

In the year 33 CE in Jerusalem, the promised Holy Spirit

descended upon the disciples, and they proclaimed the message of salvation in Jesus Christ. Three thousand were converted that day, and they were baptized on the very same day. Thus the Church was born. We read about this in the Book of Acts, chapter 2.

The Church functioned in a fluid sort of way, and a study of the Book of Acts shows there were elements of congregational, presbyterian, and episcopal forms of governance. The first leader of the Church in Jerusalem was James, the half-brother of Jesus; Peter was prominent as well.

The first problem encountered by the nascent church was that the widows from outside Judea were not being treated fairly. The apostles directed that deacons be appointed to make things right.

Next, a problem arose regarding what to do with Gentiles who were coming into the Church. Should they be circumcised and be required to obey all the Jewish laws? The issue of how to integrate Gentiles into the early Church, which had been entirely Jewish, was a major problem at that time. A decision was made, with James taking the lead along with Peter, that Gentiles would not have to be circumcised and were considered equal with Jewish believers in Jesus. The accounts of these events are all recorded in the first fifteen chapters of the Book of Acts.

Opposition arose from non-Christian Jewish leaders. The religious authorities stoned Stephen, one of the deacons chosen to help administrate equality in the Church. Persecution against the apostles drove them to leave Jerusalem and begin missionary outreaches. Early tradition tells us that they travelled widely to establish churches.

At first, the Romans considered the Christians to be a sect of Judaism, and thus they were granted protection. However, this changed as Rome began to see the Christians as a threat, because they acknowledged Jesus Christ as Lord rather than the emperor in Rome. Christianity was declared illegal. The first empire-wide persecution of the Church took place under Domitian toward the end of the first century. John the Apostle, for example, was exiled to the Island of Patmos off the coast of Turkey around 90 CE, where he wrote the Book of Revelation and perhaps also the Gospel of John.

The early Christians never went to war with anyone; they loved their enemies; they were martyred by the thousands; and yet the message of Jesus spread worldwide.

In the initial years of the fourth century, the Roman Emperor Constantine was converted to Christ. Christianity was then made legal and was even the preferred religion, and thus the Christians were no longer persecuted. This was both a good and a bad development for Christians. The Church now had power, which was misused for centuries. That abuse eventually led to the dreaded Inquisition and later to the Protestant Reformation in the early part of the sixteenth century. Power, combined in both church and state, corrupted both but especially the church. This is one reason why American Christians and others stood for the separation of church and state in the formational years of this country.

A COMMON DENOMINATOR

Any institution involving human beings is bound to be flawed. This is true of religious institutions as well. More than that, it will become corrupt in even the smallest gatherings, whether mosque or church congregation. The Bible says it this way: "For all have sinned and fall short of the glory of God" (Romans 3:23).

When a religion is spread by the use of force, intimidation, and coercion, it requires the same methods to sustain it. This inspires fear rather than true faith. The Church has learned this lesson through the painful mistakes of past centuries. Could it be that now it is Islam's turn to learn this lesson?

FOUR

LESSER JIHAD

Recently, the imam at a nearby mosque spoke with our Study of Islam class and was adamant that ISIS, Boko Haram, Al-Shabab, and other violent Muslim groups are not truly Islamic. He said that Islam is "the religion of peace."

He confirmed what I have read elsewhere: the greater, or first, form of jihad is to work against wrong by words and peaceful deeds. It is understood as a personal struggle to make oneself a more pure adherent to Islamic practice. I have found that as one gets older and more aware of the world, there is more focus on greater jihad for most Muslims. Many mature believers see the error of violent jihad, while recognizing that the Qur'an and the *hadith* do allow for it, and even demand it.

At the same time, the *salafi* movement, or Islamic fundamentalism, is promoting lesser jihad, which is a commitment to violence, insisting that those who do not share that commitment are not true Muslims.

A CALL TO RADICALISM

Perhaps young Muslims are radicalized when they are taught that only the weak fail to engage in violent jihad against the kafir, the apostate, and the infidel.

I would like to think that violent jihadists are in the minority, and are mostly young idealists who have yet to grasp the higher calling of respect, honor, and love. Or perhaps they are those living in deplorable conditions with nothing but a bleak future ahead, who burn with anger and hatred.

Here are some verses from the Qur'an that speak of something other than a personal struggle for purity.

> *Remember thy Lord inspired*
> *The angels (with the message):*
> *"I am with you: give*
> *Firmness to the believers:*
> *I will instill terror*
> *Into the hearts of the Unbelievers:*
> *Smite ye above their necks*
> *And smite all their*
> *Finger-tips off them."*
> (Qur'an Al-Anfal 8:12)

> *But when the forbidden months*
> *Are past, then fight and slay*
> *The Pagans wherever ye find them,*
> *And seize them, beleaguer them,*
> *And lie in wait for them*
> *In every stratagem (of war);*
> *But if they repent,*
> *And establish regular prayers*
> *And practice regular charity,*
> *Then open the way for them:*
> *For God is Oft-forgiving,*
> *Most Merciful.*
> (Qur'an At-Tawba 9:5)

> *Fight those who believe not*
> *In God nor the Last Day,*

Nor hold that forbidden
Which hath been forbidden
By God and His Apostle,
Nor acknowledge the Religion
Of Truth, (even if they are)
Of the People of the Book,
Until they pay the Jizya
With willing submission,
And feel themselves subdued.
(Qur'an At-Tawba 9:29)

Therefore, when ye meet
The Unbelievers (in fight),
Smite at their necks;
At length, when ye have
Thoroughly subdued them,
Bind a bond
Firmly (on them): thereafter
(Is the time for) either
Generosity or ransom:
Until the way lays down
Its burdens. Thus (are ye
Commanded): but if it
Had been God's Will,
He could certainly have exacted
Retribution from them (Himself);
But (He lets you fight)
In order to test you;
Some with others.
But those who are slain
In the way of God, —
He will never let
Their deeds be lost.
(Qur'an Muhammad 47:4)

Prophet! Strive hard
Against the Unbelievers
And the Hypocrites,
And be firm against them.
Their abode is Hell, —
An evil refuge (indeed).
(Qur'an At-Tahrim 66:9)

There is a *hadith* from Sahih Al-Bukhari, Vol. 9, Book 84 #57 that reads: "Whoever changed his Islamic religion, then kill him." (Also see Qur'an An-Nisa' The Women 4:89.)

The above words are purported to come from the mouth of Muhammad. Muslims who leave Islam or even behave in a manner considered un-Islamic are to be killed. It is likely that the motive is to cast terror into the hearts of Muslims, who must answer to a powerful leadership motivated to protect the honor of the community and of Islam generally.

Telling Headlines

For more than a decade now I have been reading of violent jihadists killing enemies, other Muslims, civilians, and women and children by the thousands. Many were not enemies, but simply innocents who did not believe that Muhammad truly represented Allah. Children—even the unborn—have been murdered, because they **could not** believe, due to their age. There is more to this than religious zeal. Only hate, anger, hopelessness, and self-loathing could drive people to commit such unspeakable acts. Such barbarity can drive people crazy; both the victim and perpetrator are destroyed.

"Let there be no compulsion in religion." So says Qur'an Al-Baqara 2:256. Yet there is compulsion for both Muslims and non-Muslims, all of which is sanctioned in the Qur'an.

Are we to believe the imam who calls the beheadings ("smite at their necks") un-Islamic? Or, are the violent jihad-ists interpreting the Qur'an more accurately in their call for attacks against the infidels? Sorrowfully, the evidence is clear; for years now I read it every day in the morning headlines and see it on television and the internet.

"The religion of peace?" Is peace achieved when apostates are murdered and unbelievers are forced to convert to Islam against their will? Can someone find faith in Allah and desire to devote his whole being to his worship while a knife is pressed to his throat?

Violent enforcement of religious tyranny is difficult to defend as a righteous practice. The radicals and extremists insist that in order to believe in Muhammad and the Qur'an, lesser jihad is absolutely mandatory. Other Muslims reject violence and declare it to be un-Islamic. Who can give the final word?

If Allah wills, reason will prevail.

ABROGATION

In a recent discussion with a scholarly Muslim whom I consider a friend, the subject of abrogation came up. He began to tell me that the lesser jihad material in the Qur'an was set aside, superseded, or abrogated by verses that speak kindly and peacefully about the "people of the book," and indeed all peoples.

I responded that the kindly words about Jews and Christians were given early on in Mecca, while the harsh words were given later in Medina. Does abrogation work forward in time as well as backward?

Perhaps abrogation does not function according to a linear time-line, with a before-time and an after-time. If not, on what basis is abrogation justified? Can anyone abrogate in support of any position, or is there a finite set of commonly agreed upon abrogations that all Muslims adhere to?

Or is it the case that abrogation is a tool that works hand in hand with *taqiyya*, as a means of preserving the honor of Islam by putting forth any argument—regardless of truth— that is expedient in any given situation?

FIVE

THE MERCY, GRACE, AND COMPASSION OF ALLAH

ALLAH THE MOST MERCIFUL, THE MOST COMPASSIONATE, THE MOST GRACIOUS

Words like those above are often found in the Qur'an. Sura 1 (Al-Fatiha) reads:

In the name of God, Most gracious, Most Merciful.
Praise be to God,
The Cherisher and Sustainer of the Worlds;
Most Gracious, Most Merciful;
Master of the Day of Judgment.
Thee do we worship,
And Thine aid we seek.
Show us the straight way,
The way of those on whom
Thou hast bestowed Thy Grace,
Those whose (portion)
Is not wrath,
And who go not astray.

It is evident that it is claimed for Allah in the Qur'an that he is merciful, compassionate, and gracious. Yet, indications from current extreme Islamists is that the only Muslim who can be assured of forgiveness and know he or she will enter Paradise is the one who dies as a martyr. Even still, Allah may change his mind. There is no assurance of salvation and forgiveness in Islamic sacred books. The scale of good works versus bad works is a scary thought to any self-aware person who is mindful of his or her crazy thoughts and desires. After all, Allah is said to know all the thoughts and desires of the heart and mind.

Mercy, compassion, and grace, as commonly understood in the Bible, have to do with forgiveness and loving kindness. Below I lay out what Biblical Christian loving forgiveness looks like.

WHAT IS LOVE?

Love can be defined in many different ways. From the Greek language as found in the New Testament, there are three terms for love: *eros*, *phileo*, and *agape*.

Eros is erotic love, which focuses on that which is strictly of an earthly nature, e.g., the love of music, art, literature, sex, and much more. It is earth bound and is easily corrupted.

Phileo is brotherly love—the love for family, friends, or a spouse, and it is also earth-bound and can be corrupted.

Agape is what the Bible refers to as the love God has for human beings, those who are **made in his image**. *Agape* is the kind of love that interests us most. The love God has for us cannot be corrupted.

In the book of Genesis in the Bible, the only created beings that spoke with and walked with God were the humans, Adam and Eve. Such interchange could occur because Adam and Eve were created in God's image, and thus they could have a relationship with Him. God loved them and they loved God. He continues to love humans with agape love. God loves the praise and worship that we direct toward him and expresses his love for us in his desire that we be with him forever in Paradise.

The Bible is filled with expressions of God's love for humanity, but we will limit our examination to a select few passages.

John 3:16

For God so loved the world, that he gave his only Son, that whoever believes in him should not perish but have eternal life.

This is probably the most well know verse in the entire Bible. Why? Because it presents the essential truth that we are actually loved by our Creator. And this shocks us, since we usually feel we are not loveable.

1 John 4:7–12

Beloved, let us love one another, for love is from God, and whoever loves has been born of God and knows God. Anyone who does not love does not know God, because God is love. In this the love of God was made manifest among us, that God sent his only Son into the world, so that we might live through him. **In this is love, not that we have loved God but that he loved us and sent his Son to be the propitiation for our sins.** *Beloved, if God so loved us, we also ought to love one another. No one has ever seen God; if we love one another, God abides in us and his love is perfected in us.* [Emphasis added.]

My favorite verse is 10, which I have bolded above. It shows that God's love is based on grace and mercy and not on our ability to love God. We are loved, and that is that.

Also in verse 10 is the word "propitiation," which means that God has acted to remove our sin to satisfy his own requirement. Our efforts at forgiving ourselves are fruitless and impossible. No amount of good work, even dying for the cause of God, could do that.

At the heart of Christianity is that Jesus died in our place and took upon himself all our sin—past, present, and future. Amazing grace! The sinless died for the sinner. This is propitiation.

Unstoppable Love

One born of God cannot ever be unborn. We like to say, "Once saved, always saved," since it emphasizes the fact that our salvation, the sure promise of heaven, cannot by any way or means be taken away. Paul the Apostle put it this way, first in Romans 8:35–37:

Who shall separate us from the love of Christ? Shall tribulation, or distress, or persecution, or famine, or nakedness, or danger, or sword? As it is written, "For your sake we are being killed all the day long; we are regarded as sheep to be slaughtered." No, in all these things we are more than conquerors through him who loved us.

If that were not clear enough, Paul continued with Romans 8:38–39:

For I am sure that neither death nor life, nor angels nor rulers, nor things present nor things to come, nor powers, nor height nor depth, nor anything else in all creation, will be able to separate us from the love of God in Christ Jesus our Lord.

Grace

God expresses his love for us by giving us his grace. Grace is God's free gift of forgiveness and salvation. Grace gives us what we could never earn, despite our best efforts. We don't have to die for the name of Christ, since that would be a work, and no one is saved by works. Here is Ephesians 2:8–9:

For by grace you have been saved through faith. And this is not your own doing; it is the gift of God, not a result of works, so that no one may boast.

Grace and faith are both gifts—God giving us what we do not deserve and cannot earn, and all because he loves us. No boasting on our part about our righteous deeds and how fervently we praise his Name takes the place of his free gift. This is love.

If Allah Wills, the grace and love of God will be upon us and in us forever and ever.

LOVE AND FEAR

A sharp contrast between Islam and Christianity has to do with love versus fear.

We do not easily identify fear in ourselves. One way to spot it is to examine the role of hate in our lives. We will hate what we fear. If we are afraid of a particular race or people group, we will often harbor hatred toward them. If we are afraid of a particular belief system or religion, we will hate those who are committed to that religion, and this begins at an unconscious level.

There are Christians who hate Muslims, because they fear them. There are conversely Muslims who hate Christians, because they fear them.

One of the hopes in writing this book is that fear and hate between Muslims and Christians will diminish, allowing us to examine sensitive issues with an assurance of mutual respect. We Christians are commanded to love those who hate us, because "God so loved the world."

FEAR IN ISLAM

As part of my research on Islam I have compiled a list of

things that Muslims fear:

- The Day of Judgment
- Going to hell
- Evil and Satan
- The jinn, bad angels, curses, and spells
- The West or Western culture
- Women
- Being considered weak or apostate
- The leaders at the local mosque
- Not being sincere enough
- Not performing rituals properly
- Allah, who can lead astray
- The internet
- Education
- The Qur'an
- Thinking independently or questioning Islam

Due to fear, many Muslims seem trapped in denial. In Western countries where Muslims are exposed to or have easy access to news broadcasts and other forms of media, they may have to keep what they learn to themselves, and cover up their knowledge.

Often Muslims are afraid to investigate and find things out for themselves, and it could be dangerous to question a religious leader. Learning is fraught with fear.

FEAR IN CHRISTIANITY

Scripture teaches that Christians need not fear the devil, the demons, or anything else. Christians do not fear those who consider them enemies, but are taught to pray for and love their enemies.

Christians do not fear going to hell, because Jesus has rescued them from hell and given to all believers in Jesus the assurance of heaven. Nothing at all can separate the Christian from his love. Nothing in all creation can take away from the security we have in Christ.

The apostle John writes, "There is no fear in love, but perfect love casts out fear. For fear has to do with punishment, and whoever fears has not been perfected in love" (1 John 4:18).

Thus for the Christian, it is God's love that allows us to remain invulnerable to fear.

Six

OBEDIENCE

THE FAITHFUL ARE OBEDIENT

Obedience to Islam is fulfilled in one's performing the five pillars, reciting daily prayers in the mosque if one is nearby, and faithfully practicing the main ordinances of the religion.

Islam is all encompassing; all of one's life is bound up in being a good Muslim. There is no division or separation between secular and religious life.

One can have the appearance of obedience in the sight of the ummah, the community of Muslims. Yet one's behavior does not always truly reflect the attitude of the mind and heart. Could one appear obedient on the outside yet have serious misgivings or even faithlessness inside? All religious faiths, including Christianity, are aware of the possibility of faithlessness taking the appearance of piety, because we can't see inside someone's heart.

LOVE VERSUS FEAR

What motivates obedience? Is it love for God or fear of God? The answer to this question makes a world of difference.

Is it possible that some Muslims are obedient not out of love but out of fear? Is there not reason to fear considering the following:

- The *ummah* and one's own family may react strongly if one does not perform religious duties as expected.
- One must not become weak in one's belief.
- One must submit to the wishes of the father, or the husband if a woman, or be in danger of actions taken for the sake of family honor.
- One must be careful to ward off *jinn* and the influence of Satan.
- Ultimately, one may go to hell and not Paradise, since one could be led astray or deceived, even by Allah himself.

There is a host of fears that may motivate some Muslims to keep up the appearance of obedience.

Christian Obedience

Christians are also called to obedience, living a life that is pleasing to the Lord our God. However, the Christian's obedience is not based on fear but on love toward God for the grace and mercy received.

We remain ever aware that before we were brought to faith, we were lost and condemned to hell. The situation was hopeless, until Jesus took all our sin—past, present, and future—upon himself. He died the eternal death in hell that we deserved, so that we would not have to suffer the consequences of our own sin. "In this is love, not that we have loved God but that he loved us and sent his Son to be the propitiation for our sins" (1 John 4:10). Propitiation means that Jesus completely satisfied the legal and spiritual demands of God for us on the cross.

While we were rebelling, sinning, and blaspheming, God forgave it all because of what Jesus did on the cross. He then went to hell, triumphed over the devil and all the demons, returned victorious, and saved us from all sin and hell.

Based on this mercy, this grace, this love, we are called to follow Jesus. This is why Christians study the Bible so much, and why the life of Jesus is so important to us. We read what he did and what he said. We learn what true obedience means, which can be summed up in the great commandments: Love God with all our heart, mind, and strength, and love our neighbor as ourselves.

Christian obedience is based minimally on performing rituals, that is, doing required things. It is more a matter of the heart and mind. Willing actions naturally follow from the inner attitude of the heart.

Christians do not need to do things to protect themselves from evil. Jesus has defeated all the demonic powers, including the chief of demons, Satan. Christians do not practice magic, spells, and curses. We do not seek to know the future, since all the future we need to know is in the Bible already. We do not need to wear or keep amulets or talismans in our homes, including the evil eye, which is merely ineffective magic. We have a much more reliable power in the precious blood of Jesus, which protects us against all evil.

Christians do not fear demons or bad angels. Biblically speaking, there are no such things as bad angels; they are merely demons in disguise.

Through his disciples Jesus casts out demons even today. I have been involved in this kind of ministry, have seen hundreds of demons cast out of hundreds of people, and continue to provide this service today.

Lastly, Christians do not, and should not, fear what the Christian community thinks or does. Though pastors and members of churches care about the welfare of their congregants, salvation is not tied to a church, institution, family, or community; Jesus alone is Savior. I have been a part of a number of different denominations, and for a long period was independent. Many Christians are not part of any named church or denomination, yet because they follow Jesus, they obey him and have no fear regarding their salvation and eternal home.

Real obedience for the Christian is based on what God in Christ has done for us out of his boundless love. We are drawn, not driven, on the basis of grace alone, which inspires us to believe, which in turn inspires us to obey.

If Allah wills, our external acts of obedience will reflect a heart truly motivated by the love of God.

IS CHANGE POSSIBLE?

Early in the Meccan period, before Muhammad immigrated to Medina, he espoused non-violent confrontation with those who opposed him. This is evident in Qur'an An-Nahl 16:125–128. But when opposition to Muhammad's message emerged in Medina, then defensive fighting was permitted. This is evident in Qur'an Al-Baqara 2:191.

Eventually, defensive fighting was not enough, and while in Medina, Muhammad received commands from Allah to fight **all** unbelievers, including Jews and Christians. This is evident from Qur'an At-Tawba 9:5 and 29. These verses received in Medina came later than the more peaceful passages received in Mecca; they thus abrogate the non-confrontational passages.

Based on the Qur'an, therefore, it is Islamic to engage in violent jihad.

PROGRESSIVES

"Progressives" is one of several terms used to describe Muslims who hope to live in peace and avoid direct confrontation with non-Muslims. These Muslims are mostly, though not entirely, found in Western countries. They may engage in the "greater" jihad, but want to live in peace.

The problem, however, is that the radicals in local Muslim communities wield power, and progressive Muslims may be intimidated by those who are intent on carrying out violent jihad. Presently, life is difficult for Muslims who wish to live in peace and harmony with those of other faiths.

APPEAL

Is violence warranted as retaliation for what the Christian crusaders did 1,000 years ago? Violence in the present day is never justified by pointing at abuses Muslims suffered centuries ago. We must live in the present and face today's realities with compassion and reason.

Is the Muslim understanding of jihad changing?

SEVEN

GETTING TO HEAVEN

My prayer for you is that we will both be in the Paradise of Allah together.

THE JESUS CONTROVERSY

Qur'an An-Nisa' 4:157 reads, "They said: 'We killed the Messiah Jesus, son of Mary, the messenger of God.' They did not kill him, nor did they crucify him, but the likeness of him was put on another man (and they killed that man)...."

The idea that Jesus was not crucified was held by Gnostics living in the Arabian Peninsula centuries before the days of Muhammad. This teaching, called Docetism, holds that Jesus only appeared to be crucified, but someone else died on the cross in his stead. This is a fundamental belief of Islam. Muhammad believed it, since that is the story he was taught from early childhood.

THE CENTRALITY OF THE CROSS

In Christian thinking, Jesus is the perfect, sinless Lamb of God, who died in our place on the cross. Since sin results in death and hell, God demonstrated his love for us when all our sin was placed on his perfect sacrifice. Jesus took our sin upon himself on the cross and literally died for us.

Christianity is the only religion in which we find God humbling himself unto death—even death on the cross—so that humankind can live eternally with him in Paradise. On the third day after his crucifixion death on Friday he rose from the grave on Sunday. This is why "there is salvation in no one else, for there is no other name under heaven given among men by which we must be saved" (Acts 4:12). One who is "saved" has assurance of entry into everlasting Paradise with God.

John the Apostle wrote, "The blood of Jesus his Son cleanses us from all sin" (1 John 1:7b).

What Jesus did on the cross is often referred to as "The Atonement," meaning the sacrifice of Jesus—the shedding of his blood that covers, or atones, for our sin.

THE ONLY WAY TO HEAVEN

In Qur'an 4:157, Jesus is referred to as "Messiah Jesus." The Qur'an is right to call Jesus "Messiah." Messiah is from the Hebrew *meshiach*, meaning "anointed one." The Greek translation is "Christ." The Messiah has been understood from ancient times as one who was to be born as a man and die for the sins of the people.

Here is what the Jewish prophet Isaiah said about the Messiah some 750 years before the birth of Jesus: "...because he poured out his soul to death... yet he bore the sin of many, and makes intercession for the transgressors" (Isaiah 53:12).

This is all because of his great love for us. "God shows his love for us in that while we were still sinners, Christ died for us" (Romans 5:8).

No one and nothing can take that salvation away, not even our own sin or stupidity. Once having been saved, we have an unshakeable assurance that we will spend eternity in Paradise with God.

WORKING FOR HEAVEN

All the world's religions except Biblical Christianity are

works-oriented, that is, salvation and everlasting life depend on what a person does and does not do, and on what a person believes and does not believe.

One thinks of the scale—more good deeds than bad deeds, which is not very reliable. Of course, dying in jihad is said to yield paradise automatically. Can one be sure? Who said so, other than the current crop of internet jihad recruiters? Is that reliable, something to base your whole eternity upon?

If I do one good thing today, I am doing well; but in my mind I fail miserably, because I cannot control the bad thoughts that come nonetheless. What a horrible predicament!

No one can earn heaven. No one; it is impossible. We can only be given eternal life in paradise as a gift. This is what Jesus Christ is all about. He gives us life. He is the Way, the Truth, and the Life. Simple as that.

If Allah wills, we will be together in heaven.

Contrast

Islam's Paradise
and
Christianity's Heaven

Paradise and heaven mean the same thing, but there is an immense difference between how Muslims and Christians view it.

Islam's Paradise

Paradise for Muslims is pictured as an oasis where there is plenty of shade, water, food, and beautiful women. This makes sense, in that Islam developed in the desert regions of Arabia.

Islamic heaven is essentially a continuation of life on earth but with great benefits, luxuries, and pleasures. Life goes on for an indeterminate amount of time, but it may not be eternal.

Christian Paradise

The paradise found in the Bible is not of this world. Instead, there exists a new heaven and a new earth, and the old heaven and old earth are dissolved. Biblical paradise is eternal—never ending.

When Christians enter paradise, we receive new bodies made for eternity. We get a glimpse of those bodies in the accounts in the Gospels in which the resurrected Christ appears to his disciples and interacts with them. Using Jesus' so-called "glorified body" as a forerunner of what we can expect of our own, we find that the new body is not subject to the limitations, nor the decay, of our earthly bodies.

In heaven, Christians come into the very presence of God, face-to-face. There is no more dying, pain, or mourning. Jesus even tells us there is no marrying in heaven. We will find wonderful worship, purposeful service, and reigning together with God forever and ever.

EIGHT

THE CHRISTIAN WEST

Islam strives to triumph over the Christian West, as well as over all other lands and people who are not submitted to Allah and Islam. This is clear and evident and is acknowledged by all Muslims.

Yet this assertion begs the question: Is the West actually Christian?

The largest single western nation, America, was founded primarily by Christians escaping religious persecution in Europe during the seventeenth and eighteenth centuries. However, not all who crossed the Atlantic were Christians.

Although many Christian and Biblical principles are built into the U.S. Constitution, such as freedom of religion, America is not a Christian nation. America as a society is becoming less and less Christian, meaning less genuinely Christ-centered and Bible-believing. True Christians, among others, see the spiritual and moral decay in American culture and are dismayed.

While there are millions of Christians in America, there are also millions of Americans who are not Christian. Where I pastor in Mill Valley, California, there are more Buddhists, atheists, and neo-pagans such as Wiccans and shamans than there are Christians. Easter Sunday is traditionally a day when most Christians go to a church of some kind. However, in Mill Valley less than 2% of the population attends a church of any kind on Easter. There are almost as many Muslims as Christians now in Mill Valley.

THE GREAT SATAN

The term "great Satan" is used to garner anger and hatred toward Americans in response to the moral laxness that has spread across the land. Muslims the world over read of crime, drug addiction, alcoholism, divorce, sexual addiction, rampant lawbreaking, and fraud. Such depravity leads Muslims to call America the great Satan. Certainly, many Christians readily agree that Satan is busy destroying lives in America. However, this does not make America itself the Satan. Rather, America is an open society, and therefore prone to influences from many sources, including evil ones.

America has chosen a representative form of government rather than some form of autocratic structure, wherever on the fascist to communist scale. The American people themselves decide, through the electoral process, who will govern. It is a risky form of governance, because things can go wrong, but Americans prefer to live in messy freedom than orderly tyranny.

Americans enjoy a separation of church and state. The state seeks to curtail the kind of evil that harms others' lives and property through the rule of law. There is no law against burning a Bible. One need not fear arrest for attacking Jesus or calling him any name under the sun, nor is there much of an outrage when it happens—and it does happen. There is no blasphemy law.

SHOCKING?

After years of research into Muslim-majority nations, and in speaking with former and present Muslims, I have found that there is as much sin in those countries as there is in America. The difference is that it is not reported in the daily news media but slips under the radar; it is imperative to shield from public knowledge those acts that could cause shame to the family, ummah, or nation. However, the reality is that all humans are sinners.

Many of the sins found in the West also afflict Muslim-majority countries: drug and alcohol abuse, along with the exportation of drugs and the raw materials for drug production; financial corruption, especially where there is a gross disparity between the rich and the poor; murder excused as honor-keeping, with the victims being mostly women; murder of apostates and non-believers; racial prejudice; sexual immorality of all kinds. A past leader of Iran said, "There is no homosexuality in Iran." However, rape of women, girls, men, and boys occurs. Those with the power and the proclivity to do so use their victims as sexual slaves.

We in America have had to acknowledge that these occurrences are widespread in our own country. That awareness leads to our dealing more honestly with the problem. More honesty might help Muslims oppose similar practices rampant throughout their nations as well.

FOR ALL HAVE SINNED

The fact is that people everywhere on the planet have a sin problem. "For there is no distinction: for all have sinned and fall short of the glory of God" (Romans 3:22b-23).

Sin is an age-old problem from the earliest days of humanity. In the sixth century BCE, the prophet Jeremiah said, "The heart is deceitful above all things, and desperately sick; who can understand it?" (Jeremiah 17:9).

Americans, Europeans, Africans, South Americans, Iranians, Saudis, Pakistanis, Egyptians, and Syrians—all people of all religions and races without exception—are guilty. To conceal sin problems and proclaim purity and guiltlessness when it is not true only leads to more sin.

ROMANS 6:23

I am a sinner saved by graced. The difference after salvation is that I am more conscious and sensitive than ever before to things that are not right before God. Yet I still find myself missing the mark in many ways.

The Christian Scriptures provide great hope for all peoples of the world, Muslims included. The Apostle Paul, a terrible sinner, actually arranged for the murder of Christians before his conversion. After his conversion he was staggered to find out that God still loved him. Here is what he said about it:

For the wages of sin is death, but the free gift of God is eternal life in Christ Jesus our Lord. (Romans 6:23)

If Allah wills, all peoples of the world will discover the key to overcoming sin.

HOMOSEXUALITY

This is a most sensitive subject, but I think it must not be ignored.

Muslims reject homosexuality. It is haram, meaning forbidden; yet various sources report it is widely practiced among Muslim men. (I do not know if Muslim women experience or engage in it as well.) Islam denounces homosexuality, but it is nevertheless practiced, though not broadcast like homosexuality is in Western countries. Both Shi'a and Sunni Muslims have told me the very same thing—many Muslim men have practiced or continue to practice it.

PRACTICING BUT NOT IDENTIFYING

In sharp contrast with gays in America, the majority of Muslims practicing homosexuality are not actually homosexuals, nor do they identify with the lifestyle associated with Western homosexuality. What then is going on?

Is it possible that hormone-driven young men direct their lusts where they can—that is toward each other—because of the strict prohibitions against associating with women outside of marriage? Also, many young Muslim males have a difficult time finding wives for various reasons, including that older men may have more than one.

THROWING THE FIRST STONE

In chapters 7 and 8 of John's Gospel we find the story of a woman caught in the act of adultery. She was brought to Jesus by the religious authorities to see what he would do.

It is probable that the authorities used the situation in order to test Jesus. The law said that the penalty for adultery was stoning to death (Deuteronomy 22:13–21). Would Jesus uphold the law or not?

Jesus addressed the crowd, "Let him who is without sin among you be the first to throw a stone at her" (John 8:7). To the credit of those present, they all turned away and went home. Jesus then asked the woman, "Woman, where are they? Has no one condemned you?" Jesus then said, "Neither do I condemn you; go, and from now on sin no more" (John 8:10–11).

Jesus called her behavior sin. He knew human weakness and understood like no one else on earth the dreadful consequences of the power of sin. Jesus loves the sinner and only wants to see that sinner forgiven and cleansed. Jesus said,

> *"Come to me, all who labor and are heavy laden, and I will give you rest. Take my yoke upon you, and learn from me, for I am gentle and lowly in heart, and you will find rest for your souls. For my yoke is easy, and my burden is light."* (Matthew 11:28-30)

NINE

ABOUT EVIL

Although both Islam and Christianity take the devil seriously and neither questions his existence nor that of demons, there is a startling difference between the jinn, bad angels, *Iblis*, and *Shaytan* of Islam, and the demons and Satan of the Bible.

One difference is that there are no "bad angels" in the Bible—only demons, which are fallen angels. There is one Satan, or devil, and a myriad of demons who follow his lead and are under his control.

In Islam, not only are there bad angels, but there are also five classes of demons, and these beings have considerable power.

FOLK ISLAM

The actual practices of Muslims in many parts of the world are in some ways distinct from Islam's official doctrine. While wandering through the Grand Bazaar in Istanbul, Turkey, I came upon shop after shop offering occult objects for sale, such as the evil eye, thought to protect from the jinn. This is one of a myriad of examples of folk Islam.

Occult practices entered into Islam at its very inception in the seventh century and were not all the result of recitations given to Muhammad, though some were. Some of the magical devices originated from and became practiced through the influence of the Sufis. Muslims often use occult means such as sorcery, fortunetelling, witchcraft, spells, curses, amulets, and charms to protect themselves from evil powers and to obtain spiritual help, especially for healing illnesses. It is not an exaggeration to say that folk Islam is dominated by fear of evil powers.

Like Roman Catholics' prayers to departed saints, Muslims also appeal to dead and living Islamic saints for help, which constitutes another form of occult practices—spiritism—and by that I mean contact with angels, demons, and spirits of the dead.

Much of Islamic worship consists of ritual prayers. Great stress is laid upon performing the rituals correctly, in the fear that if they are not conducted perfectly, they will be ineffectual. In this way, the practice of Islam devolves into superstition and the daily prayers into something resembling magic spells.

Even the Qur'an has become somewhat of a magic charm for many Muslims. For most Muslims, little is known of the Qur'an outside of the prayers memorized in Arabic (the language of only 20% of Muslims worldwide), and these can become little more than appeals for protection from evil. The ablutions made before prayer in the mosque are sometimes viewed as washing away demonic influence.

Even more serious is the belief that when one is born, a "familiar spirit" of the opposite sex is born at the same time but is the offspring of Satan. This being is thought to become a "bad angel" that sits on one's left shoulder, balanced by a good angel on the right shoulder, both of whom one may appeal to during one's lifetime.

A GREAT OBSTACLE FOR MUSLIMS

One of the great obstacles to safety in Christ is that Muslims must deny that Jesus was crucified. Their position is nearly identical to the Gnostic denial of the crucifixion referred to as Docetism. (Docetism taught that someone who looked like Jesus was crucified on the cross and not Jesus himself or generally, that it only "seemed" that Jesus was crucified.)

It was prophesied in the Old Testament (see Psalm 22 and Isaiah 53) that the suffering servant of Israel, otherwise known as the Messiah, would come and redeem his people. Then the actual event took place, and Jesus became a "curse" by taking our sin upon himself. Deuteronomy 21:22–23 reveals that someone hanged on a tree is cursed by God (also see Galatians 3:10–14). Jesus became a curse for us; he received the penalty of sin on our behalf when he hung on the tree, the cross of Calvary. Jesus' blood cleanses from all sin (see Colossians 1:15–20).

Because of Jesus' victory over sin, we have victory over Satan and his host of demons. Without that we are vulnerable to the hateful and murderous wiles of the devil.

BIBLICAL DEMONOLOGY

In the Christian Bible there is a devil named Satan, which means "adversary." There are demons, which are fallen angels who took Satan's side in a rebellion against their Creator. This Satan was in the Garden of Eden and enticed Adam and Eve to break God's single law. Eve ate first of the forbidden fruit, then Adam followed, and Satan gained an entrance into human history.

Right after Jesus' baptism, as he began his ministry, the Holy Spirit drove Jesus into the desert to be tempted by Satan. For forty days the temptation continued, and each time Jesus defeated the devil by appealing to the Word of God.

Early in his ministry, Jesus cast demons out of those possessed or demonized. At a synagogue in Capernaum, a city near the northwestern tip of the Sea of Galilee, Jesus encountered a man who had a demon. Here is the story:

> And immediately there was in their synagogue a man with an unclean spirit. And he cried out, "What have you to do with us, Jesus of Nazareth? Have you come to destroy us? I know who you are—the Holy One of God." But Jesus rebuked him, saying, "Be silent, and come out of him!" And the unclean spirit, convulsing him and crying out with a loud voice, came out of him. (Mark 1:23–26)

It must be noted that the unclean spirit, the demon, knew who Jesus was. Demons always know who Jesus is and also know that the Holy Spirit of God indwells followers of Jesus. The demons not only know who Jesus is, but they know they are under his power and authority; Jesus can cast them into hell. Demons do not fear people, but they fear Jesus for this reason. Hundreds of thousands of Christians have learned this to be true in real time and space down through the centuries. This is not so in Islam.

Jesus taught, healed people, and cast demons out during his entire ministry. He turned no one away but welcomed and received the outcasts—the demon possessed who had been driven out of their minds. Those with horrid diseases like leprosy, who were declared to be unclean and dangerous, he received with open arms.

At one point Jesus sent his disciples out to minister and gave them this charge: "And he called the twelve together and gave them power and authority over all demons and to cure diseases, and he sent them out to proclaim the kingdom of God and to heal" (Luke 9:1–2).

At another time, as recorded in Luke chapter 10, he sent out seventy-two others. When they returned from their missionary journey they reported, "Lord, even the demons are subject to us in your name!" (Luke 10:17). And then, lest these missionaries think too much of themselves, Jesus warned,

"Do not rejoice in this, that the spirits are subject to you, but rejoice that your names are written in heaven" (Luke 10:20).

The book of Acts records that the early Christians, including Paul, did cast out demons. For centuries later, followers of Jesus commonly cast out demons, until, unhappily, the Roman church corrupted the ministry of casting out demons, and it became a magical kind of exorcism. However, the casting out of demons continues unabated until this day, a fact to which I can personally attest.

Two passages follow, both from the Apostle John's first letter:

> *The reason the Son of God appeared was to destroy the works of the devil (1 John 3:8).*

> *He [Jesus] who is in you is greater than he who is in the world (1 John 4:4).*

The simple truth is that Jesus is more powerful than the devil, and Christians need not fear demonic mischief in their lives, because of the finished work of Jesus.

In my book, *Deliver Us from Evil: How Jesus Casts Out Demons Today*, I describe the work of casting out demons, based primarily on my personal experience. After seeing hundreds of demons cast out of hundreds of people, I can testify to the fact that Jesus casts out demons even today. It is a rather simple and common ministry that any Christian can conduct; frankly, however, few do.

If Allah wills, we will not live in fear of forces that have no power over us.

The Ultimate Goal

An examination of the differences between the ultimate goals of Christianity and Islam reveals a dramatic contrast in worldviews and mindset. Ultimate goals define our purpose and attitude in life, and this can provide useful insight.

"Islam Will Dominate the World"

The above slogan appeared recently on a number of placards carried by devout Muslims in a demonstration in an English city.

On the CBS news program *60 Minutes* that aired Sunday, June 14, 2015, the ultimate goal for Islam was clearly presented, leaving no doubt in anyone's mind as to what the religion's aim is: world domination achieved by whatever means required.

This goal is stated in the Qur'an and cannot be disputed or treated symbolically; it is and has been understood thus by Muslims who take their faith seriously since the seventh century.

While the majority of Muslims prefer to live and let live peaceably, Islam is not democratically administered but is controlled by powerful radicals who believe that in order to please Allah and copy the agenda of Muhammad, Islam must conquer all peoples of the world.

The so-called "extremists" are actually the only ones who honestly represent Islam's objective. Those who struggle to characterize the goal of Islam within a politically correct framework show their naiveté, indeed disingenuousness, at this point in history in failing to face this issue head on.

CHRISTIANITY WILL NOT DOMINATE THE WORLD

The goals of Christianity are different from those of Islam.

Jesus commissioned his followers to go into the entire world and proclaim the Gospel message. If the message is not received in one area, we are to move on to new areas.

Our goal is simply proclamation. We are witnesses to who Jesus is and what he has done; we are not judges, jurors, or enforcers. Jesus also made it clear that those who become his followers would be few in number (see Matthew 7:13–14).

The Church is to preach the cross of Jesus and leave the results to the inner working of the Holy Spirit. Indeed, there can be no compulsion of religion in Christianity. Faith in Jesus comes strictly by hearing the message of Christ; "So faith comes from hearing, and hearing through the word of Christ" (Romans 10:17).

It must be admitted that in the past some Christian organizations have tried to force people to convert, be baptized, and join a church, even though it is actually impossible to force someone to become a Christian. Those methods were misguided, regrettable, and ineffectual in the long run. True Holy Spirit conversion is a matter of the heart and mind, with the Holy Spirit bringing about a transformation from the inside out.

In the Book of Revelation we read that the Christian Church will suffer persecution and defeat throughout history.

The worst of this is to occur just before the end of the age, which could be any time now. When Jesus returns to gather together his Church on that last day, the Day of Judgment, he will be triumphant for all the world to see; he is the conquering Champion of God.

TEN

WOMEN IN ISLAM

In Islam, women are not seen or treated as the equals of men.

QUR'AN, HADITH, AND SHARIA LAW

In Qur'an Al-Baqara 2:282, we find that two women are needed to be a witness, but only one man is necessary.

Part of Qur'an Al-Nisa' 4:3 reads: "Marry women of your choice. Two, or three, or four." Muhammad had twelve wives, but only four are granted to Muslim men, and fewer if they are not able to care for them. In Muslim-majority countries and elsewhere, parents arrange marriages, and the women have no say in the matter.

Qur'an 4:11 states that a woman gets half the inheritance a man receives:

> God (thus) directs you
> As regards your children's
> (Inheritance): to the male,
> A portion equal to that
> Of two females: if only
> Daughters, two or more,

Their share is two-thirds
Of the inheritance;
If only one, her share
Is a half.

Qur'an 4:12 offers more inheritance details that further establish the Muslim view of the inequality of men and women.

Qur'an 4:34 begins with the statement that men are the protectors and maintainers of women. Then the tone changes in regard to women who do not measure up for one reason or another:

As to those women
On whose part ye fear
Disloyalty and ill-conduct,
Admonish them (first),
(Next) refuse to share their beds,
And (last) beat them (lightly).

(Note: Words such as "first" and "lightly" that are bracketed in the above passage are added by editors.)

Qur'an Al-Nur ("Light") 24 contains instructions about dealing with those who commit adultery and fornication. If a woman is found guilty of either, she must be publically flogged or whipped with 100 lashes.

Qur'an 24:2 states, "Flog each of them with a hundred stripes: Let not compassion move you."

Qur'an Ar-Rahman 55 speaks of the pleasures of paradise, and verses 56–57 indicate that in paradise a man may expect sex with beautiful, chaste (virginal) women. Islamic paradise is characterized by a fulfillment of male sexual desires.

Keeping women in a second-class and inferior status is what pious Muslims believe is proper. They do not see any virtue in the equality of women with men.

For some Muslims a marriage may not actually need to be a love relationship. Indeed, a man and a woman who fall in love after a period of getting to know each other is rare. Dating is not allowed in much of the Islamic world, and when practiced it is considered weakness bordering on apostasy. Since early in the history of Islam, the practice has been for families to arrange marriages.

The view of women in *sharia* law, whether of the Hanafi, Maliki, Shafii, or Hanbali orthodox schools, may be summarized as the following: Women are considered of less value than men in regard to inheritance, their witness in a legal trial, and wages given for work, among other areas. Often they cannot appear in public without proper covering and/or without a male escort, who should be a husband, son, brother, or other male relative. This is because women are said to be in danger of leading men astray with their sexuality.

Commonly, women are told they are the "gems" of the family and thus need to be protected. Could it be that this notion is actually enabling a policy of domination rather than a cherishing of women?

KHADIJA AND HER UNCOVERING

In many Muslim countries, even where Muslims are a minority, women must completely veil themselves in public or at least wear a *hijab* (a head covering like a scarf).

The authority for this goes back, according to some, to a story from the life of Muhammad regarding his first wife Khadija (from *The Life of Muhammad* by Ibn Ishaq, translated by A. Guillaume, published by Oxford University Press, page 107). The story tells us that Muhammad was so unsure of the nature of the being who had been communicating the Qur'an to him that he was terribly troubled, even to the point of considering suicide. Khadija convinced him that it was the angel Gabriel and not a jinn or Satan who had been appearing to him in the cave on Mount Hirah.

Khadija devised a test for Muhammad. She asked him to sit on her left knee (or thigh), then her right, and then on her lap. Each time she asked him if he saw the angel Gabriel. Each time he said yes. But when Khadija revealed herself by disrobing and again asked Muhammad if he still saw the angel, he said no. The idea was that only an angel from Allah would flee from such sinfulness as the sight of a naked woman. The angel appearing to Muhammad would clearly be evil if the sight of an unclothed woman did not trouble it.

Based, at least partly, on the story of Khadija and her unveiling, women must cover themselves. Others say the reason women must cover themselves is to honor Allah. Maybe both are correct.

FEMALE GENITAL MUTILATION (FGM)

Below is a description of FGM from Wikipedia:

The procedures differ according to the ethnic group. They include removal of the clitoral hood and clitoral glands (the visible part of the clitoris), removal of the inner labia and, in the most severe form (known as infibulation), removal of the inner and outer labia and closure of the vulva. In this last procedure, a small hole is left for the passage of urine and menstrual fluid, and the vagina is opened for intercourse and opened further for childbirth. Health effects depend on the procedure, but can include recurrent infections, chronic pain, cysts, an inability to get pregnant, complications during childbirth, and fatal bleeding. There are no known health benefits.

The story about Khadija in the previous section reveals fear of the power of the nakedness of women, which contributes to the age-old practice of female circumcision. The rationale behind FGM is that the sexual drive of women must be curbed by making sexual intercourse painful. It is said that men would only want to marry circumcised women, because they can then trust them not to wander.

There are generally five reasons why Muslims practice female genital mutilation. First, as stated above, is to limit and control a woman's sexual drive and thus assure she will be a virgin when married.

Second is hygiene. It is thought that the female's genitals are unsightly and dirty. Sometimes women who are not circumcised are considered unfit to handle food and water.

Third, FGM is a necessary condition for a woman to be considered complete. The parts removed are considered vestigial male parts, and thus should not be part of a woman's anatomy.

Fourth, FGM is seen among some Muslims as a rite of passage, an initiation into adult womanhood, giving a woman the cultural identity of her community.

Fifth, Muslims did not invent FGM; pagans, Jews, and Christians have practiced it, although it is not a condoned religious practice for either Jews or Christians.

It should be noted that nowhere in the Bible is there FGM. It seems to be an ancient expression of men's fear of women.

FGM is not practiced by all Muslim communities (Islamic apologists claim only a minority), but the practice is still common today, almost always performed by older women who had the same done to them as children. Many secular and Muslim women are speaking out against FGM, and laws are slowly being passed to outlaw the practice.

RAPE

While FGM is either obligatory (Shafi'i school of Islamic jurisprudence) or recommended as "praiseworthy" (Maliki school) under Islamic Law, rape and sex slavery of females seized in war is recounted with approval in the Qur'an (Q 4:24; Q 33:50), the *hadith*, and *sira* (biographies of Mohammad). While the term for rape is not used directly, the idea is certainly clear: women taken as captives in war, especially non-believers, are subject to the whims of their captors.

WOMEN IN PARADISE?

Paradise is supposed to be granted to those whose good deeds outweigh their bad deeds.

Some Muslims say that only a virginal woman can go to paradise. The Qur'an assures that all the women in paradise will be beautiful and virginal. Does this mean that a non-virgin woman cannot go to heaven? And would this disqualify all married women? Is it possible Allah does not intend paradise for most women, but only women who die in jihad?

The bridge over hell, across which all must walk to reach paradise, is said to be narrow and precarious. Some also claim that men jostle women off so they fall into hell, and in some *hadith* are indications that most of those sent to hell by Allah will be women.

AN ASSURANCE

Here is what Jesus said: "For this is the will of my Father, that everyone who looks on the Son and believes in him should have eternal life, and I will raise him up on the last day" (John 6:40).

Jesus' "everyone" includes women, many of whom followed him during his earthly ministry. Jesus treated women with compassion and high regard to a degree that even exceeded the Jewish culture of his time. He treated women as equal with men to receive salvation and sit at his feet as disciples. At least four women observed his crucifixion and resurrection. In the letters of Paul we find many women who were followers of Jesus. In the Church today are many thousands of women who serve as pastors, elders, preachers, teachers, and missionaries.

The Bible says all of us, men and women, have sinned and broken God's law and are thus in need of being rescued from an eternal hell: "For the wages of sin is death, but the free gift of God is eternal life in Christ Jesus our Lord" (Romans 6:23).

On the cross, Jesus suffered and died for men and women,

taking all their sin upon himself and dying the death we would have to die otherwise. His gift of salvation is freely given, not earned. It is not a question of doing more good deeds than bad deeds. Think about it—can anyone's good deeds really outweigh the bad? I know for a fact that my bad deeds outweigh my good deeds. Our deeds spring from the heart and are not just what appears outwardly. Outward obedience is easy to feign. But, as the ancient Hebrew prophet Jeremiah said, "The heart is deceitful above all things, and desperately sick; who can understand it?" (Jeremiah 17:9). This basic truth applies to male and female equally.

If Allah wills, we will come to value all people, not on the basis of gender, but on the basis of God's depth of love for all of us.

THE *SIRA*

I have been reading *The Life of Muhammad*, a translation of Ibn Ishaq's *Sirat Rasul Allah*, as translated by A. Guillaume and published by Oxford University Press in 1955 and re-issued in Pakistan in 1967. *Sira* is the traditional name for the biography of Muhammad.

There are three primary sources of authority for Muslims: the Qur'an, the *hadith*, and the *sira*. From the last two authorities, but primarily the *hadith*, the *sunnah* is determined, which is the pattern of Muhammad's life: his actions, words, and manner of life.

Not all Muslims cite the *sira* as an authoritative source for information about Islam and Muhammad. Some, however, do attach considerable weight to the account of Muhammad's life.

The author, Muhammad ibn Ishaq, was born in Medina around AH 85 (AD 704) and died in Baghdad in AH 151 (AD 762). He is associated with the second generation of the pious forefathers or traditionalists.

Many passages in the *sira* prompt this appeal. Please know that it is not my purpose to defame or blaspheme Muhammad in any way but simply to inquire about the incredible nature of some of the things Ibn Ishaq has written about Muhammad. This is largely difficult for Muslims to do, even read about, because to do so could be considered "weak" by Muslim leadership.

Courageously then let us ask ourselves: Are the following accounts concerning Muhammad true and accurate?

THE NIGHT JOURNEY

Ishaq tells the story of the prophet Muhammad's night journey to Jerusalem and ascent into heaven. In this story Ishaq allows the reader to see something of his thinking. In fact, as Guillaume says in his note (page xx of his Introduction), "The story is everywhere hedged with reservations and terms suggesting caution to the reader."

And then, Muhammad's favorite wife, Aisha, reported that it was only the apostle's spirit that was transported to Jerusalem, as well as to heaven (Guillaume, p. xx). Other reports concerning the night journey reveal that in Ishaq's day the event was debated. In the end, commenters have resorted to the common "only God knows" or "God knows best." Perhaps what is said of the *hadith* is true of the *sira* also. Some *hadith* are genuine, some are good, and some are weak.

Islamic defenders say it makes no difference if there was an actual ascent into heaven or not. Even if only in a dream, still the night journey was of God.

About the tradition that Muhammad is a pure descendant of Adam, the first human, we find the phrase, "Only God knows the truth" (Guillaume, p. 4).

MOST ASTONISHING

On page 72 of Ibn Ishaq's *sira* is the story of an event that occurred to the young Muhammad. It was thought, due to some sort of illness, that Muhammad had become possessed by a demon. His mother, Amina, denied the possibility, and it was further reported that, "When she was pregnant with him a light went out from her which illumined the castles of Busra in Syria, and that she had borne him with the least difficulty imaginable."

A number of men came to Muhammad and asked him to tell them more about himself. Here is that account:

> I was suckled among the B. Sa'd b. Bakr, and while I was with a brother of mine behind our tents shepherding the lambs, two men seized me and opened up my belly, extracted my heart and split it; then they extracted a black drop from it and threw it away; then they washed my heart and my belly with that snow until they had thoroughly cleaned them. Then one said to the other, weigh him against ten of his people; they did so and I outweighed them. Then they weighed me against a hundred and then a thousand, and I outweighed them. He said, "Leave him alone, for by God, if you weighed him against all his people he would outweigh them."

Is this sort of material, resembling hundreds of other similar hero tales from that locale and era, simply a fantastical miracle legend? Mythical accounts of saints, monks, visionaries, and messiahs performing extraordinary miracles are rather typical.

I will recount only one more instance about Muhammad found in the *sira* of Ibn Ishaq, but there are hundreds more stories that could be discussed.

REPORTS OF ARAB SOOTHSAYERS, JEWISH RABBIS, AND CHRISTIAN MONKS

On page 90 of the *sira* with the above title, Ibn Ishaq writes:

> Jewish rabbis, Christian monks, and Arab soothsayers had spoken about the apostle of God before his mission when his time drew near. ... As to the Arab soothsayers they had been visited by satans from the jinn

with reports which they had secretly overheard before they were prevented from hearing by being pelted with stars.

Here "pelted with stars" is interesting, since "stars" are the objects we see in the heavens. But of greater interest is the question of whether the soothsayers—Arab fortunetellers or occult artists—had supernatural knowledge of Muhammad? The commentary goes on to describe the jinn listening in to conversations about Muhammad.

On page xix, Guillaume states, "A word that very frequently precedes a statement is *za'ama* or *za'amu*, meaning, "he alleged." The implication is that the source of the information about Muhammad may not be completely trustworthy. How reliable then are the accounts found in the *sira*?

What is the expectation for the modern Muslim or one studying Islam in reading such things? Do these writings present a crisis of plausibility? How is that which is found in the *sira* to be understood? As fact? As legend? As symbolism? As invention?

ELEVEN

MEN IN ISLAM

Most of us men, regardless of religion or culture, have a hard time talking about anything to do with love and sex. It is just how we are. Yet, these areas are such a major part of our thought lives and physical lives that we have to accept and face it. Did you know that the part of our brains that controls the sexual function is 2.5 times larger than that of women?

There is only one area of greater sensitivity, and that deals with what we believe about God. I am convinced that a mark of maturity, of being a reliable and intelligent human being, is the ability to look at reality without fear. But who can do this?

MY OBSERVATIONS OF MUSLIM MEN

For the last several months I have been attending Friday prayers at our local Sunni mosque, getting to know the imams and other leaders, and I have met a number of young men who attend regularly. A few of them remember me from my days of being the freshman baseball coach at the local high school.

These young Muslims live somewhat differently than those from their home countries of India and Pakistan. They attend public school where the girls dress in the usual Western fashion and show plenty of flesh, even if they have a head covering on. I do not, however, recall seeing any Muslim girls come to a game to watch the boys play. From what I understand, the Muslim young people do not mix much, if at all, with the other kids at school.

Ours is as liberal a town as you can imagine; Republicans are few and far between. My observation is that the local Muslim population has integrated somewhat, but the mixing of the genders in places like Pakistan, Somalia, Saudi Arabia, or Sudan is very restricted. I wonder whether the local young Muslim men are able to date Muslim girls. Do they have the chance to choose whom they want to marry? In the countries mentioned above, the girls are usually never able to meet their future husband unless he is a relative, due to the tradition of arranged marriages.

Based on my reading and on interviewing Muslim men, I keep hearing that love and sex is very different for them than for most naturalized American men. It is a scary proposition in many ways. Is marriage in Islam ever a relationship between two people who learn to love each other and desire to spend their lives together? Or is it an institution for men to have many children, especially male children, in which sex is merely for procreation?

When I consider these things, I cannot help feeling sadness for men in Islam because of all that they are missing out on in the loving, intimate bond of marriage.

DEVALUING WOMEN

Female genital excision, though not practiced in all Muslim-majority regions, is widely practiced to this day in the name of protecting a young woman's virginity and therefore her family's honor. It is performed on very young girls who are unable to make their own decisions. The procedure removes the organs of female sexual stimulation, thus greatly diminishing any enjoyment the female might have. Is her sexual pleasure unimportant? Even without the female excision, are a woman's sexual needs considered? If they are not, the male misses out. Women are reduced to being objects for the sexual gratification, or lust, of men. The result is that men in these cultures will not experience the joy of giving the pleasure of intimacy in marriage.

Do Muslim men learn to fear the opposite sex as they grow up? My impression is that they do not value women as equals but instead see them as inferior and needing protection, scrutiny, and correction, even if it must be harshly applied.

I have read that in Muslim communities, young men as well as older men might be overcome with *fitnah*. This means men may be subject to a powerful lustful desire for females, possibly triggered by the mere sight of an uncovered ankle, too much of her hand, face, or hair. The woman is held responsible for eliciting the man's lust. Women are blamed, not men.

I understand that this blame-shifting is even taken to the extreme that if a woman is raped, the rapist can claim he had a lustful fit caused by the female showing the smallest amount of skin. Her future marriage prospects will be diminished, if not eliminated, since she is no longer a virgin. It could even cost her life, since the family has been dishonored. She is considered the guilty party, not the man. What does this do to the man's conscience?

There is evidence that honor killings occur in Muslim enclaves in Western countries as well as in Muslim-majority countries. I have tried to imagine how this tragic tradition must impact Muslim males, let alone Muslim females. For one thing, I suppose it must produce enormous fear of having to appear to be in control of all the females and younger males in his family, even if he does not want that responsibility. It must produce a damaged conscience for committing, allowing, or even keeping silent during the killing. The honor killing of a daughter, wife, or mother must deeply impact the father, brothers, and other male members of the family despite the sense that the killing is to honor Allah and the umma. Silence must be kept in non-Muslim majority countries, and the trauma must sink deep into the family's psyche and be very damaging to its sense of safety and integrity.

All of the reduction in the value of women and the whole complex relationship between male and female Muslims suggests that Muslim men might have difficulty within marriage. Once the marriage has been performed, it is generally understood that the Qur'an prescribes that husbands can, or must, beat their wives, however lightly. My suspicion is that this also damages the conscience of the husband and prevents a wife from respecting her husband. She merely fears him. A relationship of mutual love and respect—the core of a good marriage relationship—would likely never develop.

Most of us have trouble maintaining a healthy relationship with someone of the opposite sex, yet we men are able to grow up learning to respect and value women. There is no such thing as a perfect marriage, and the divorce rate in Western countries is high, too high. Divorce among Muslims is rarer than among other cultures, largely due to the fact that divorce is usually only initiated by the husband—that is if he does not take a second wife. The shame and dishonor for the woman's family causes major upset and could lead to her demise, directly or indirectly.

What about men taking more than one wife? The background to polygamy has a great deal to do with survival in harsh environments such as that of Arabia where Islam was spawned. The infant mortality rate, the need to provide boys to fight for and defend the clan, and the short life span in times past are factors that forever altered the way many desert peoples think of marriage. And it has impacted Islam's thinking about marriage.

CONSIDER ANOTHER VIEW OF MARRIAGE

Here is how the Creator God intended marriage to be according to the people of the Book.

We begin in Genesis 1:27:

So God created man in his own image,
in the image of God he created him;
male and female he created them.

What is plain is that God is both male and female at once. "Image" has to do with the fact that God's desire was to communicate with and have fellowship with humans. It is not that humans look like the Creator, which would be impossible, but that they had the spiritual capacity to communicate with and have fellowship with their God.

Then we have Genesis 2:18:

Then the LORD God said,
"It is not good that the man should be alone;
I will make him a helper fit for him."

Also plainly, the male on his own was not enough; a female was necessary. Therefore, out of the man God fashioned a female, made out of the very essence and nature of the male. The man was thrilled with the woman and said:

This at last is bone of my bones
and flesh of my flesh;
she shall be called Woman,
because she was taken out of Man.
Genesis 1:23

Male and female, the same yet different—different so that the male and female could reproduce. And God created humans so that by an internal hormonal mechanism, a loving bond could develop between them—we call it love—that guaranteed offspring.

Yet there is more:

Therefore a man shall leave his father and his mother
and hold fast to his wife, and they shall become one flesh.
Genesis 2:24

One flesh (my emphasis) is the English translation of the Hebrew, which is echad. It means one unit. Though two separate persons, in marriage they are one echad or unit. That unit is the essential family structure. (The Trinity is an echad as well, three in one or one in three, as discussed in Chapter 1, Tawhid.)

One flesh is the intent of God, and that is why divorce is wrong in the eyes of God—a sin, but it is not an unforgiveable sin. I am myself a divorced man who has remarried. (In the Christian community there are many different views on divorce and remarriage.)

The Apostle Paul, in his letter to the Ephesians, discussed the core elements of marriage. He wrote, "Husbands, love your wives, as Christ loved the church and gave himself up for her..." (Ephesians 5:25).

Paul continues: "Husbands should love their wives as their own bodies. He who loves his wife loves himself. For no one ever hated his own flesh, but nourishes and cherishes it, just as Christ does the church, because we are members of his body" (Ephesians 5:28-30).

As a Muslim man, I ask you to fearlessly consider the following questions: Has Islam distorted the intent of the Creator God regarding relations between men and women? Has the original purpose of marriage been twisted?

FEAR OF WOMEN LEADS TO RADICALIZATION?

It has been noted by any number of commentators that the road to radicalization of young Muslim men begins with the place and role of Muslim women. It is taught that girls and women must be properly dressed, covering almost all of the body, with the clothing loose and flowing so not to reveal anything of the body's shape. Also, it is recommended that women stay indoors as much as possible, and when out of the home a male relative must accompany them. This results in a distorted view of women in Islam, affecting how Muslim males perceive and interact with females.

Do Muslim males carry an excessive burden of responsibility toward women? At a certain age, males in the family will accrue to themselves the job of watching after sisters, even mothers. This is bound to strain relationships within a family, and the male's view of female family members may be less than familial.

This effectively develops into a fear of women. Such fear surrounding relations with females is unequalled in any other religious group, except perhaps in ancient Judaism (long since changed). From fear, women are then demonized, and they become a group to be hated and toward whom violence may be committed. This is further justified as a means of bringing about Allah's justice, since all that happens is the will of Allah.

The point is that often the West is blamed for enticing women to be immodest and un-Islamic. So the West becomes the enemy, and the woman who reveals too much according to strict Sharia Law becomes an enemy as well. The whole situation is charged with fear, hate, and anger.

If Allah wills, we will come to value all people, not on the basis of gender, but on the basis of God's depth of love for all of us.

SEX IN PARADISE?

Jesus makes it clear that there are no sexual relations between humans in heaven. The party of the Sadducees, who denied resurrection, asked Jesus a question designed to make the doctrine of resurrection seem ludicrous. The question had to do with a hypothetical woman who'd had seven husbands, all of whom died. Then the religious Sadducees asked, ". . . [W]hose wife will she be? For they all had her" (Matthew 22:28).

Jesus replied, "You are wrong, because you know neither the Scriptures nor the power of God. For in the resurrection they neither marry nor are given in marriage, but are like angels in heaven" (Matthew 22:29–30).

There is a marked contrast between the paradise of Islam and the heaven of the Bible. In Islam, paradise is characterized by the satisfaction of human sexual needs and desires, and it is pictured as an oasis with bountiful supply. In the Bible, heaven is utterly beyond imagination, but has nothing to do with anything earthly. In heaven, women will not exist solely for the sexual pleasures of men.

SEXUALITY IN PARADISE

One of the main emphases in Islam is sex between men and beautiful, perpetually virginal women in paradise. However, the nature of these women is in doubt. How could they remain perpetual virgins, all the while satisfying the sexual desires of men? It seems that one of the pleasures of paradise is the continual deflowering of virgins. Muslim paradise seems to cater only to men.

A Muslim may be stoned to death for homosexual acts, yet things appear to change in paradise. There, according to Islam, men will also have a plentiful supply of young boys with whom to have sex. This is startling, and most Muslims would be offended if they were aware of it.

Let us look at two passages in the Qur'an:

> *Round about them will serve,*
> *(Devoted) to them,*
> *Youths (handsome) as Pearls*
> *Well-guarded.*
> (Qur'an At-Tur 52:24)

> *Round about them will (serve)*
> *Youths of perpetual (freshness),*
> *With goblets, (shining) beakers,*
> *And cups (filled) out of*
> *Clear-flowing fountains :*
> (Qur'an Al-Waqi'a 56:17–18)

The Arabic word for "youths" is *ghalman* and refers to boys who assume the feminine role in homosexual relations. *Haram*—forbidden now—yet permitted in paradise. (Alcohol is treated similarly. Forbidden now, but not in paradise as Qur'an 56:19 makes plain.)

BIBLICAL SEXUALITY

In Genesis, God told Adam and Eve to "be fruitful and

multiply" (Genesis 1:28). In order to do that they had to engage in sexual relations. Most Christians agree that the Creator God made sex pleasurable to ensure that the human race would continue. Additionally, it is a glue that holds men and women together in enduring relationships.

The Apostle Paul gives us insight into the Biblical view of how husbands should treat their wives: "Husbands, love your wives, as Christ loved the church and gave himself up for her" (Ephesians 5:25). Shortly thereafter, he continues:

> In the same way husbands should love their wives as their own bodies. He who loves his wife loves himself. For no one ever hated his own flesh, but nourishes and cherishes it, just as Christ does the church, because we are members of his body. "Therefore a man shall leave his father and mother and hold fast to his wife, and the two shall become one flesh." (Ephesians 5:28–31)

A wife is not a sexual slave or merely someone exploited to fulfill the sexual desires of the husband. The husband and wife are one—that single unit made up of two. To "love" means to care for and nurture. In the Bible the wife is to love her husband and the husband is to love his wife.

A DEEPER VIEW OF MARRIAGE

Marriage in the Christian Bible is also a symbol of something even deeper than human relationships. In Scripture, Jesus is referred to as the bridegroom and the Church as his bride. At the end of the age, Jesus, the bridegroom, comes to receive his bride, the Church. This is beautifully described in Revelation, chapters 21 and 22. It shows that the Church belongs to Christ, and the very first thing that happens on the Day of Judgment is the marriage supper of the Lamb, the "Lamb" being Jesus Christ himself (see Revelation 19:6–10).

TWELVE

THE SATANIC VERSES

According to Islamic tradition, at a time when Muhammad was having trouble converting his own Quraysh tribe to Islam, Satan spoke through Muhammad's mouth. The recitation given by the devil to Muhammad is known as the "Satanic verses."

THE BACKGROUND STORY

In the *sira* by Ibn Ishaq is the story of a compromise between the Quraysh and Muhammad. For one year Muhammad agreed to worship the Quraysh's gods, and for one year the Quraysh were required to worship Muhammad's God, Allah.

The gods that the Quraysh wanted Muhammad to worship were al-Lat and al-'Uzza. At first, Muhammad received from Allah a strong admonition to reject the invitation to worship the pagan gods of the Quraysh. Qur'an Al-Kafirun 109:1–6 expresses Allah's rejection:

Say: O ye
That reject Faith!
I worship not that
Which ye worship.

Nor will ye worship
That which I worship.
And I will not worship
That which ye have been
Wont to worship,
Nor will ye worship
That which I worship.
To you be your Way,
And to me mine.

The Quraysh persisted in trying to persuade Muhammad, yet Allah continued to warn Muhammad, as preserved in Qur'an Az-Zumar 39:64–66; Muhammad was not to worship pagan gods.

The Quraysh were still not satisfied, and Muhammad looked for a way to break the stalemate. He then received a revelation saying that is was okay to pray to al-Lat, al-'Uzza, and Manat, three female gods of the Quraysh. These pagan deities, Muhammad was told, would act as intercessors with Allah.

In Qur'an 53 (An-Najm), 19–20 we see:

Have ye seen Lat and 'Uzzat
And another the third (goddess) Manat?

In all the official versions of the Qur'an something that came next is missing. Muhammad originally followed the above verses with this:

"These are the exalted cranes
and their intercession is to be hoped for."

(Note: "cranes" is a synonym for goddesses.) These words are not to be found in modern, sanctioned versions of the Qur'an, and it is easy to see why.

There is enough evidence, mostly from *hadith*, to expose the fact that an embarrassing verse has been deleted.

At first, Muhammad ridiculed these deities. Later they were embraced for the sake of reconciling with his own tribe, which was pleased with Muhammad's change of opinion. According to Ibn Ishaq, page 166 in the *sira* published by A. Guillaume, the Quraysh were thrilled:

> Then the people dispersed and Quraysh went out, delighted at what had been said about their gods, saying, "Muhammad has spoken of our gods in splendid fashion. He alleged in what he read that they are the exalted gharaniq whose intercession is approved."

Muhammad realized he had made a mistake. He said, "I have fabricated things against God and have imputed to him words which he has not spoken" (Tabari, vol. 6, p. 109).

Muhammad was not only grieved but also fearful for having allowed Allah's message to be contaminated. The result was a stern warning from Allah as found in Qur'an Al-Isra' 17:73–75.

And their purpose was
To tempt thee away
From that which We
Had revealed unto thee,
To substitute in Our name
Something quite different:
(In that case), behold!
They would certainly have
Made thee (their) friend!

And had We not
Given thee strength,
Thou wouldst nearly
Have inclined to them
A little.

In that case We should
Have made thee taste
An equal portion (of punishment)
In this life, and an equal portion
In death: and moreover
Thou wouldst have found
None to help thee against Us!

On page 166 of the *sira*, Ibn Ishaq explains:

So God sent down (a revelation), for he was merciful to him, comforting him and making light of the affair and telling him that every prophet and apostle before him desired as he desired and wanted what he wanted and Satan interjected something into his desires as he had on his tongue. So God annulled what Satan had suggested and God established his verses, i.e., you are just like the prophets and apostles.

In Qur'an Al-Hajj 22:52 this is affirmed:

Never did We send
An apostle or a prophet
Before thee, but, when he
Framed a desire, Satan
Threw some (vanity)
Into his desire: but God
Will cancel anything (vain)
That Satan throws in,
And God will confirm
(And establish) His Signs:
For God is full of knowledge
And wisdom:

(Note that the words in parentheses are not original to the Qur'an but are added by Qur'anic scholars for clarification purposes.)

The following verse, Qur'an 22:53, continues the theme:

That He may make
The suggestions thrown in
By Satan, but a trial
For those in whose hearts
Is a disease and who are
Hardened of heart: verily
The wrong-doers are in a schism
Far (from the truth):

Allah had now relieved Muhammad of fear and also sent down another recitation by way of affirmation in Qur'an An-Najm 53:19–23:

Have ye seen
Lat, and 'Uzza
And another,
The third (goddess), Manat?
What! For you
The male sex,
And for Him, the female?
Behold, such would be
Indeed a division
Most unfair!
These are nothing but names
Which ye have devised,
Ye and your fathers,
For which God has sent
Down no authority (whatever).
They follow nothing but
Conjecture and what
Their own souls desire!
Even though there has already
Come to them Guidance
From their Lord!

The Quraysh proceeded to use all of this to attack Muhammad and to question him about the verses from Satan. For these tribesmen, the issue was, can Muhammad's revelations be trusted?

How can one be certain Satan did not place other passages in the Qur'an? Certainly, most Islamic scholars deny the legitimacy of the Satanic verses as did Ibn Ishaq, yet not all do.

A critic might easily question whether the appearance of the Satanic verses in the Qur'an could be fabricated by later corrupt copyists. However, there is no indication that enemies of Islam inserted them into the text of the Qur'an. The fact is that for centuries faithful Muslims accepted them as true and genuine.

The Master's Voice

Edits have occurred within the Christian Bible, including deletions and passages added through the centuries. We are aware of these changes due to the abundance (approx. 5,000) of New Testament manuscripts extant. Yet the essential message of the Bible prevails, and we marvel at the consistency of the voice of God coming through his words from the very beginning (Genesis) to the very end (Revelation).

In the Christian faith, we learn to discern the sound of Jesus' voice amidst the confusion and din of voices coming at us from the world, from inside our own minds, and from the enemy of God. We are able to do this because of the presence of the Holy Spirit within us, guiding and teaching us. Jesus tells us, "My sheep hear my voice, and I know them, and they follow me" (John 10:27).

If Allah wills, we will pray for and receive a gift from God that enables us to distinguish the voice of God from unholy voices.

IS MUHAMMAD WORSHIPED AS A GOD?

No images or pictures of Muhammad may be made. To do so is haram—forbidden.

The second commandment in the Bible prohibits making images or idols for the purpose of worshiping them as gods:

> *You shall not make for yourself a carved image, or any likeness of anything that is in heaven above, or that is in the earth beneath, or that is in the water under the earth. You shall not bow down to them or serve them, for I the LORD your God am a jealous God.* (Exodus 20:4–5)

It is *haram* to make an image, or picture, or any other representation of Muhammad. However, it seems to me that Muslims have elevated Muhammad to the status of God.

Additionally, the pious forefathers copied and emulated all that Muhammad did and said, which may be understood as a form of worship. Further, it is *haram* to speak a word against Muhammad.

The third commandment in the Bible is, "You shall not take the name of the LORD your God in vain, for the LORD will not hold him guiltless who takes his name in vain" (Exodus 20:7).

Again, for the Jew and Christian, a parallel implication is that the prohibition against taking Muhammad's name in vain elevates him to the status of God.

WORSHIP OF JESUS

Christians openly worship Jesus Christ as God. Christians do not consider this to be idol worship or pagan polytheism. Jesus said, "I and the Father are one" (John 10:30). This "one" is a unity of three: Father, Son, and Holy Spirit.

Worship of images and other man-made objects is forbidden in the Ten Commandments, but Christians do not complain when images are made of Jesus, because we do not worship the images themselves. They are just pictures or representations that tell a story and serve as reminders of the God we love.

Christians do not react prohibitively when others burn or desecrate images of Jesus. We may find it improper or disrespectful, but we do not seek to punish or kill the perpetrators. We realize that such offenders are not endowed with faith in and love for the one they desecrate.

I personally would not make any images of Muhammad, because I know it would be insulting to Muslims. However, what are we to make of Muslim retaliatory attacks on those who do make images of Muhammad? Does it not suggest a certain weakness, as though Islam cannot bear up under any foolish attempts at ridiculing it? Why the need to turn to violence?

Muhammad is seen by Islam as the perfect person, correct in all things, without blemish. He is more than a warner, an apostle, or a messenger. Reverence for him and for his status of perfection approaches that reserved for God.

Is Muhammad worshipped? If so, doesn't this make Islam polytheistic?

THIRTEEN

READING THE CHRISTIAN BIBLE

During ten years in Christian theological seminaries I attended classes devoted to the study of Christian-based cults and sects, such as Mormonism, Jehovah's Witness, Christian Science, Unitarianism, and dozens more. There were also classes on the major world religions, such as Hinduism, Buddhism, Islam, Baha'i, and Shamanism. Neither the professors, the denominations running the schools, nor the churches involved were the slightest bit concerned about impressionable young students learning about conflicting world religious views. In fact this was encouraged and expected.

One would hope that the same would be the case in places of learning and training for other faiths as well.

A CORRUPT BIBLE?

Often I have read material published by Muslims claiming that the Bible has been changed or corrupted to the point that it is not close to the original manuscripts.

Christians have long studied the Bible, asking hard questions about the content. Scholars have devoted their lives to getting as close as possible to the original writings of both Old and New Testament.

I have taken courses in theological seminaries wherein week-by-week we worked with Hebrew and Greek manuscripts. One of my favorite things is to look at critical examinations of Bible texts in order to examine the historical support given to various renderings. The science of critical examination of the approximately 5,000 extant manuscripts of the New Testament is so advanced that it is no exaggeration to say that we can rely on modern texts of the Greek New Testament to be accurate within 95% or better.

All of the 5% of variations are minor in nature. It boils down to issues such as, does the best manuscript use the name "Jesus," or "Jesus Christ," or "Christ," or "Lord Jesus Christ," or "Lord Jesus"; and of course it does not matter in this case which is the correct reading, since we know of whom the text is speaking. It is safe to say that no doctrine hangs on any of the variants.

Additionally, all the variants are known. We can study them, and they are open to all. The study of the variants is merely interesting; a Christian's faith does not hang in the balance.

Christians have two "words." One is the written word, the Bible, and the other is the living Word, Jesus himself. In the written word we see the living Word, and that leads Christians to love the Bible, because it tells us about Jesus.

Certainly, Christians vary on how we see certain points of doctrine. However, on issues where we find differing opinions, we mostly agree to disagree.

A PURE QUR'AN?

Muslims claim the Qur'an is pure and without error.

My study of the Qur'an, as well as the *hadith*, even the *sira*, gives me pause. In this era when considerable attention has been given to the Qur'an, there are some serious concerns.

I am wondering if many Muslims believe the Qur'an is

pure but have never read it. Many non-Arabic speakers have memorized vast portions of it, yet they often do not know the meaning of the Arabic passages.

Is the Qur'an therefore used magically, almost like an amulet? Is a printed copy sacred? Should someone be punished, even killed, if a copy of the Qur'an is mistreated?

Over the years I have thrown out many Bibles, sometimes when they have become worn out or when I began using a translation I liked better. It is a unique book, but just a book, and there is nothing sacred about the physical pages. It is the living Word, Jesus, who counts. Christians do not worship the Bible but the Lord whose story, teaching, and person are found there.

Worldwide scholars—Muslim, secular, and of other religions—are examining the Qur'an in detail at this very moment. This cannot be stopped or prevented. Not all will consider the writings that Islam holds as sacred to be so, just as they do not all hold that the Bible is holy and the Word of God.

Free people must decide for themselves what is true and what is false. We must have the courage to read, examine, and question—everything.

If Allah wills, you will study the books for yourself; read the Bible and read the Qur'an. Make a fearless examination of both. Ask God to reveal the truth to you as you go along. This cannot hurt but only help; it is not a trivial pursuit.

VISIT A CHURCH?
VISIT A MOSQUE?

May a Muslim visit a church? I can confidently answer yes to this question, based on the fact that there have been two imams, a Sunni and a Shi'a, who have visited my church. They accepted my invitation to speak at our Islamic Study Class in 2015. We did not meet in our chapel but in our fellowship hall. On both occasions the session concluded with a prayer. To the best of my knowledge, no one was offended, nor were any religious faith practices violated.

Recently I contacted a local mosque that I was not familiar with, and in answer to my query of whether I could attend the Friday meeting I was immediately given a positive answer.

I have been attending regularly now, speaking with Muslim men gathered there following the time of prayer. Several know me now and seem to feel comfortable with my presence. I take off my shoes, sit in a chair in the back, and pray in my own way. It is important to demonstrate that I respect their faith practices.

Happily, there is no contrast here.

As an appeal, I wish to suggest that people of different faith positions need not fear each other. We do not have to agree, but we can acknowledge our common humanity, our common seeking after God, and our mutual respect, indeed love, for those who share the planet with us. After all, we are all created by God.

Let's not be afraid to learn something of what others hold dear. So much of hate is based on ignorance or founded on news reports. Not that there is nothing to fear—there is—but it need not always be that way. Mutual cooperation and understanding can go a long way to bringing civility, even temporal peace.

Fear is an enemy that needs defeating. Fear produces anger and is behind so much of the hate we see in our world. Fear is very dangerous. Christians are wrong to fear and hate Muslims. The reverse is true as well, and I do not know where the greater wrong exists. This is why I appeal to Christians and Muslims to get to know what makes one another tick; get to know Muslims, you Christians, and get to know Christians, you Muslims. What a difference that will make!

FOURTEEN

LEAVING ISLAM

Christianity does not rise or fall monolithically if someone in the church leaves. False conversion, i.e., a person being in a Christian church without actually being born again of the Spirit of God, is an issue I have researched for decades. As a long time evangelical pastor, I can tell you that a high percentage of people in sound Bible-preaching, evangelical churches, through no fault of their own, are not actual Christians but have merely been Christianized.

As a pastor I have seen countless church members come and go, and there is nothing to gain in trying to restrain them. We trust that God's elect will find their way to a church that will nurture their faith. As for the nominal Christian, we leave the question of their conversion to God, praying for them and allowing them the freedom to leave if they wish.

Dear Muslim reader, if you wished, could you leave Islam?

What would be the consequences should you decide to stop attending the mosque, and if you are a woman, to take off the *hijab*, stop praying the *salat* prayers, and simply cease practicing Islam?

This is a most difficult question, because leaving Islam

could mean serious trouble and loss of almost everything, even your life.

To be weak is only a step away from being *kafir*, even a *shirk*. If your weakness or softness toward Islam were deemed apostasy, the consequences could be the worst.

CULT MENTALITY

For years I was part of a cultic Christian group. One day a professor of theology told me that the group I was with was cultic. I reacted in horror and brought the professor a copy of our group's statement of faith. "That is not the problem," he said, "it is the way you see yourselves and others that is the trouble."

He pointed out that the cultic mentality is not reserved for religious groups alone, but political, economic, and psycho-therapeutic/educational groups as well. When the religious and political are combined, then this opens the door for a particularly toxic mindset.

Whatever the name of the group is, whatever its goals are, regardless of how much power and prestige the group has, what matters is how the group views itself and others. Typical of a cult are notions such as these:

- Outsiders and unbelievers are perceived as being in error, and deceived by Satan, and deserve to be treated harshly and even eliminated.
- The group's truth is considered the only truth, and the falsehood of other groups needs to be squashed.
- Outsiders are to be feared, despised, avoided, and scandalized.

There are a number of Bible-based Christian groups that fit this category. I am a Baptist pastor and am aware that there are even some Baptist churches that fall into the category of cultic.

IS ISLAM A CULT?

Perhaps in a nation where Islam is dominant, it is difficult for a person to leave Islam, even if he or she is an atheist inwardly. In a nation where Islam does not dominate—perhaps a Western country where a person lives in a tight-knit community of Muslims—what then? Even this situation presents difficulty for the one who wishes to leave Islam. Where is the freedom to choose for oneself?

From my research, I have come to realize that some Muslim people wonder if they should or if they can leave Islam.

If Allah wills, the God who created you and loves you will be your guide as you consider these difficult questions.

A CALL TO REFORM

Christianity went through a major reformation in the six-teenth century called the Protestant Reformation, out of which have arisen hundreds of new denominations. Since that time, no single entity dictates what everyone holds as an unchangeable view on Christianity, yet the core truths of the Gospel are not changed.

Islam has not experienced a reformation; in many ways it is still operating as though this were still the seventh century. There is little room to debate, question, or critique anything to do with Muhammad, the Qur'an, the hadith, or even traditions that developed from ancient cultures. Despite the different camps—Sunni, Shia, and Sufi—it is as though thinking were frozen in time.

I believe that a majority of Muslims are open to the possibility of reform in Islam. They are yearning to be free of repressive control, and desire to live and let live. I am not advocating an abandonment of Islam; I am suggesting that a stand be taken against inflexibility and intolerance of dissension.

A practical way to take a stand for reformation is for Muslims, especially the men, to protest the killing of innocent civilians, whether they be other Muslims, Christians, or any population.

Why shouldn't you take to the streets with marches, placards, and flyers, or to the Internet and other digital and broadcast media in the name of the majority of moderate Muslims, demanding a stop to atrocities committed by the minority in the name of Islam? (Some Muslims have already begun this form of protest in the wake of the Paris and Brussels tragedies.)

Christians are content to live in a world where we do not dominate. We do not insist that the world live under the dictates of a Christian power structure. Around the world, in the face of ever-increasing hostility from Muslim extremists and even from the secular culture, we continue to speak about Jesus Christ and His simple message of love and grace.

When will moderate Muslims tire of the chafing yoke of extremist leadership? Could Islam experience a reformation?

Who among you will take a stand?

FIFTEEN

WHO IS JESUS?

Over the course of my research I have gained some under-standing of Muhammad and Islam. During this time of study I have come to respect and appreciate Islam and the Muslim people, whereas before my studies I was affected by daily news reports about Islamic extremists that uncon-sciously created a fear, anger, and even hatred for Muslims.

Now I love, pray for, and reach out to Muslim people. If I had been told of my present mindset two years ago, I would not have believed it.

For the Christian, it is a high expression of love to tell oth-ers about Jesus. Therefore, as an expression of love I am going to end this small book with what I consider a proper conclu-sion: presenting who Jesus is and what he did, using his own words.

THE SEVEN "I AM" SAYINGS

In the Gospel of John, Jesus made seven statements begin-ning with the words, "I am." Each of them tells us something important about Jesus. Illuminating them is a daunting task, as theologians have produced large volumes on each of them.

Still, I think that even presenting the highlights is an effective way to discuss Jesus, my Lord and Savior.

MOSES, BURNING BUSH, AND TETRAGRAMMATON

First, let's look at the origin of the phrase, "I am."

In chapter 3 of Exodus is the story of God sending Moses to the Egyptian pharaoh to ask for the release of the Hebrew slaves. While Moses is caring for a flock of animals in the desert, he happens upon a bush that is on fire but is not consumed by the fire.

As Moses approaches, God (*Elohim* in the Hebrew text) calls out to him. What follows is God's command for Moses to go to Pharaoh. Moses mildly protests and wants to know the name of the "god" speaking to him. Apparently, at this point Moses was a polytheist and thought this "god" must have a name to distinguish him from other gods.

Elohim's answer is mysterious and somewhat of a riddle, for he says his name is YHWH (or Yahweh with vowels added). This name is known as the Tetragrammaton, meaning "four letters." Notice what *Elohim* says to Moses:

> God also said to Moses, "Say this to the people of Israel, 'The LORD, the God of your fathers, the God of Abraham, the God of Isaac, and the God of Jacob, has sent me to you.' This is my name forever, and thus I am to be remembered throughout all generations." (Exodus 3:15)

In the text above, LORD is YHWH and is the name of God forever.

Definitions of YHWH have been several: "I am that I am," "I am," "I will be who I will be," and similar designations. Essentially, Yahweh cannot be contained in a name such as Baal, one of the ancient names for a god in the region of Canaan. The God speaking to Moses is the ultimate and only God. Moses became a monotheist.

YHWH or Yahweh is translated in the Greek version of the

Hebrew Bible known as the Septuagint or LXX as Ego Eimi or I, I am.

Jesus referred to himself as "I," or "I am." In doing so he associated himself with the ancient and timeless God who revealed himself to Moses at the burning bush.

There are seven "I, I am" sayings in John's Gospel, plus one additional time when Jesus uses the Tetragrammaton in John. In every case it is *ego eimi*, with *ego* being the personal pronoun, first person singular, meaning "I." The *eimi* is the present indicative first personal singular (a subject nominative and without any sense of time, thus timeless) meaning, "I am." To translate *ego eimi* in a most literal manner one arrives at "I, I am."

I AM THE BREAD OF LIFE

Bread, the staff of life, is an old expression for food and sustenance, for without bread life ends.

> *Jesus said to them, "**I am** the bread of life; whoever comes to me shall not hunger, and whoever believes in me shall never thirst."* (John 6:35) [Bold emphasis added.]

Jesus is like bread and water, necessary for life, and in this case, Jesus is essential and necessary for eternal life.

Jesus is not speaking literally, though some have taken it so; rather the Eastern mindset sees it as a metaphor. (The Western mindset is more prone to take it literally.) The Bible, like the Qur'an, is an Eastern document.

I AM THE LIGHT OF THE WORLD

> *Again Jesus spoke to them, saying, "**I am** the light of the world. Whoever follows me will not walk in darkness, but will have the light of life."* (John 8:12)

Darkness is a metaphor or symbol for evil and sin. Light

is the symbol for holiness and truth. Jesus is, in himself, that light, that holiness, that truth.

I Am the Door of the Sheep

Sheepfolds were fenced, with one gate or door. The shepherd stood by the door and counted the sheep as they entered for the night. There was only one way in. Sheep could not jump or climb over the wall or fencing. The shepherd would not allow in any other creature.

> So Jesus again said to them, 'Truly, truly, I say to you, **I am** the door of the sheep. All who came before me are thieves and robbers, but the sheep did not listen to them. I am the door. If anyone enters by me, he will be saved and will go in and out and find pasture." (John 10:7–9)

"Saved" is the key word here. The word is not warned, guided, taught, enlightened, or directed; it is saved.

"Saved" means to have the Savior rescue you, forgive all your sin, and give you the gift of eternal life. This is God's free gift of grace, because poor, powerless, and dumb sheep cannot save themselves.

I Am The Good Shepherd

The shepherd leads the flock, and Christians are likened to a flock of sheep. Of course, sheep are not too bright, are easily led astray, and are open to attack by wild beasts.

Jesus is not only the shepherd, he is the good shepherd. There is a bad shepherd, which Jesus calls a "thief," saying,

> The thief comes only to steal and kill and destroy. I came that they may have life and have it abundantly. **I am** the good shepherd. The good shepherd lays down his life for the sheep. (John 10:10–11)

Then and now, shepherds must protect their flocks from

being ravaged by thieves and other marauders. A shepherd could be killed as a result.

Jesus lays down his life for the sheep. This is a clear reference to the cross where Jesus laid down his life by taking our sin upon himself and dying in our place.

I AM THE RESURRECTION AND THE LIFE

Lazarus and his sisters Mary and Martha were friends of Jesus. Lazarus became sick and died. When Lazarus had been dead four days, Jesus arrived at Bethany, the little village two miles from Jerusalem where the family lived. In a conversation with Martha, Jesus said to her,

> *I am the resurrection and the life. Whoever believes in me, though he die, yet shall he live, and everyone who lives and believes in me shall never die. Do you believe this?* (John 11:25–26)

Jesus made the most incredible claim: "I am the resurrection and the life." No one else could ever say that, nor has anyone ever made such a statement. Jesus said it, and backed it up by raising Lazarus from the dead, causing such a problem for the religious leaders that they sought to kill Lazarus to shut him up.

Life in paradise and rescue from hell depends solely upon Jesus. He alone took our sin away and was buried, thus putting away sin forever. Then he rose from the grave. He is alive forever more and will come again at the end of the age, on the Day of Judgment, to receive to himself in paradise all those who believe in Him.

I AM THE WAY, THE TRUTH, AND THE LIFE

> *I am the way, and the truth, and the life.* (John 14:6)

It has been said that either Jesus was an outrageous liar, he was crazy, or he told the absolute truth.

Anyone who studies Jesus in the Gospels will tell you Jesus is no liar. They will tell you he is the most sane and rational person imaginable. Examining Jesus for ourselves makes all the difference. Clearly it takes courage to do this. When I attempted this myself back in 1963, I was afraid of what I might find. What if I were wrong! It would be embarrassing, at minimum.

Let others scoff, criticize, intimidate, ridicule, threaten! To avoid the study of Jesus and his life on earth is to miss too much; it is to miss out on all that is of actual importance.

I AM THE TRUE VINE

"Vine" is a metaphor for the nation of Israel as found in the Old Testament. Associated metaphors are "vineyard," and "fig tree." Jesus said,

> *I am the true vine, and my Father is the vinedresser.*
> (John 15:1)

Jesus, himself, is Israel and the Church. Israel and the Church are words that mean the "People of God."

Jesus is the head of the Church, which is his body. Upon conversion, by the power of the Holy Spirit, each one who is born again is placed into Christ Jesus.

Jesus is the vine. The Father is the vinedresser, similar to being the shepherd of the flock.

BEFORE ABRAHAM WAS, I AM

When Jesus was teaching at the Temple in Jerusalem, some of Judaism's leaders accused him of having a demon, and he said to them,

> *Truly, truly, I say to you, before Abraham was, **I am**.*
> (John 8:58)

"I am"—*ego eimi*—was the one who addressed Moses out of the burning bush. Abraham lived twenty centuries before Jesus, yet Jesus says he lived before Abraham. The wording of this statement means that Jesus has always lived, that he is ageless and eternal.

The Father, the Son, and the Holy Spirit—the Trinity—this is who God is. Thus did Jesus identify himself. No matter what anyone says about him, however demeaning or however fraudulent, it changes nothing. God does not cease to be God because someone doesn't believe or understand that truth.

A FINAL NOTE

If you, dear reader, are Muslim, please take the time to study Jesus. Find out for yourself. You have nothing to lose but everything to gain.

You may pray and ask God, Allah, to reveal the truth to you. God will hear the prayer, "Is Jesus really the I am?"

The ancient prophet Jeremiah said, "You will seek me and find me, when you seek me with all your heart" (Jeremiah 29:13).

If Allah wills, you will seek God with all your heart, and you will find him.

www.ingramcontent.com/pod-product-compliance
Lightning Source LLC
Chambersburg PA
CBHW032138040426
42449CB00005B/303